INSIDE GAME DESIGN

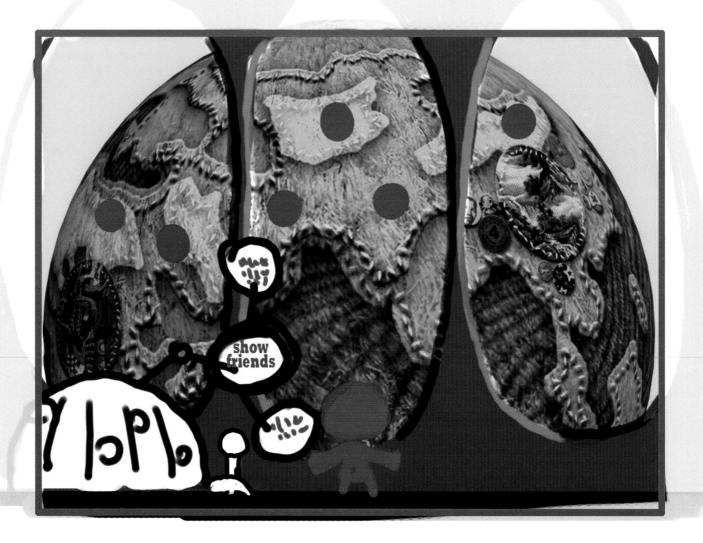

INSIDE GAME DESIGN
IAIN SIMONS

LAURENCE KING PUBLISHING

LAURENCE KING

Published in 2007 by
Laurence King Publishing Ltd
361–373 City Road
London EC1V 1LR

Tel: +44 20 7841 6900
Fax: +44 20 7841 6910
email: enquiries@laurenceking.co.uk
www.laurenceking.co.uk

A catalogue record of this book is available from the British Library.

ISBN 13: 978-1-85669-532-9
ISBN 10: 1-85669-532-8

Designed by Hoop Design

Printed and bound in China

Cover: Animation editing using Motion Builder and mo-cap footage
from *B-Boy*™. © 2006 Sony Computer Entertainment. Developed by
FreeStyleGames.

Frontispiece: Development sketch by Kareem Ettouney and Mark
Healey of Media Molecule for *Little Big Planet*. Image reproduced by
kind permission of Sony Computer Entertainment Europe.

For Sarah Simons –
she only really *likes*
'bust-a-move', but I still
love her.

CONTENTS

INTRODUCTION

Increasingly, the gap between mainstream culture and videogame culture is less about levels of consumption, and more about levels of understanding. We know that the games industry enjoys huge commercial success, but it's not always clear what the value of it is in anything other than financial terms. Videogame evangelists are often eager to claim that the industry is now 'Bigger than Hollywood!', but they seldom take the time to explain why it's more *interesting* than Hollywood. A lack of cultural confidence abounds. Despite being one of the fastest growing, most complex, sometimes celebrated and frequently sneered-at forms of modern culture in the developed world, videogames remain poorly understood by the masses. Commentary about videogames tends to be limited to the surface of the games themselves, with discussion about process, context, method and motivation being limited to the narrow margins of the specialist press.

If these amazing things contain a fraction of the potency we're led to believe they do, surely we need to know more about where they came from? Who and where are these people, these companies that make these things? What are their lives like? Why are they bothering? What are they going to make next? How and why are they making these things? Maybe if we could understand them more, we wouldn't be as suspicious or afraid.

But videogames are complicated. One of their defining characteristics is the breadth of their form. This is both the most exciting and the most dangerous thing about them – they confound lazy assumption. Ask a random selection of people to tell you what they think of when you say 'videogame' and you'll receive a radical variety of answers. The illicit pleasures of *Grand Theft Auto: San Andreas*; the photo-real carnage of *Gears of War*; leaping around the room with *Wii Sports*; the complex delights of a flight simulator; the audacious visceral pleasures of *God of War;* and at least one person will be thinking of *Tetris* (or *Pong* – always *Pong*). In their genre, aesthetic and form, videogames are an incredibly diverse area of media. When we consider them it's imperative that we don't make any assumptions about what they are. Videogames are many amazing things, the least of which is consistent.

For the purposes of illustration, I'll tell you about a recent stroll I took down the aisle of a commuter train. I took the opportunity to observe the machines and their users in their natural habitat – some fieldwork.

The laptops first; there was a predictably high density of spreadsheets, Word documents and PowerPoint presentations being worked upon, but also a high number of passengers playing *Solitaire*. Along with *Minesweeper*, this is one of the core benefits of using Microsoft Windows. Although you can elect not to install these games on your machine, by default they're present. The games are as much a part of the operating system as the bugs. Bill Gates *knew* people would need a place within Windows to escape from work. These ubiquitous distractions are a necessary annex tucked away in the Start menu of the Office workstation. If you have Windows, you have games. *Solitaire* and *Minesweeper* are two of the most played videogames in the entire world, and predominantly enjoyed by people who are 'not gamers'. Of course, the modern PC can play a whole host of amazing titles, although no-one seems to be playing any today. Fans of irony will be particularly disappointed to learn of the absence of anyone playing Microsoft's *Train Simulator*.

Other passengers are more explicit in their devotion to play. They are happy to be seen using gaming devices. At least six of them have Sony PlayStation Portables, three have Nintendo DSs and all of them are plugged into their users' ears with discreet headphones. Various titles are being played, reflecting the diversity of modern game design. *Ridge Racer* is an old favourite finding new life on the PSP, while on the DS two travellers are doing mental arithmetic and other such demanding mind-games with *Dr Kawashima's Brain Training*. If ever there was a title that challenged what we thought videogames were, it was this. At a time when levels of basic literacy and numeracy in the world are apparently in decline, 2006 was the year that mathematics went mainstream in a high-street videogame.

The essential geek-chic lifestyle device, the iPod, is an obligatory companion for music-loving commuters. None of these passengers is playing games on an iPod today, although they could if they wanted to. Out of the box, iPod is supplied with games already on it. The music is extra.

The signal for mobile phones is always quite poor on this route, so most of them are rendered mercifully silent for the duration. However, all progressive owners know that communication is really just a niche function of their phones. Phones are very useful for talking on, but if it weren't for the games that are embedded in their software, the attraction would surely be severely limited. At least five commuters are engaged in a deep communion with a 'thumb-candy' game. These tightly focused pieces of software allow games to be controlled with just one digit, an extraordinary design achievement. These are the true mainstream games, the truly ubiquitous devices. A game that slots neatly into your life and makes no great demands of time or understanding from the player – it's simply there when you need it. In between meetings or waiting for a train, the mobile game can satisfy your need for a quick burst of mental stimulation, a burst of entertainment, a burst of modern playing.

Lest the more conservative reader feel that there's cause for alarm in this scene, I should make it clear that not *everyone* was playing games on this journey. There was also a high percentage of people reading quality fiction, consuming informed newspapers and magazines, opting to sleep or sometimes just to stare meditatively out of the window. But it's fair to surmise that games have nestled nicely into our lives. No longer a conspicuous and peculiar pastime exclusively enjoyed by the pale-faced male, once you begin to look a little harder you see that games are everywhere. As this short walk down the carriage demonstrates, even when not on dedicated gaming machines, videogames are present as diversions on altogether more 'serious' computers. But while videogames might be all around us, we don't always recognize them.

Videogames are different from other media, more difficult to classify. They keep reinventing themselves and shifting their forms and locations. When they were isolated in amusement arcades they could be identified and understood, but annoyingly they keep marching into new territories – onto our phones, our satellite boxes, our iPods… Frankly, it puts us innocent media consumers in a difficult position. We know what books and films are. We know how to use them. We understand where they come from and who makes them. If we want to learn a little more about a specific work, we can read literary reviews of it in the mainstream newspapers, or we can watch intelligent television programmes where clever people sit on sofas late at night and argue about them. You know where you stand with the cultural establishment, but these *videogames*…

This book isn't predicated on any particular shared definition or idea of videogames or 'gameplay' as a single *thing* that can be understood. In the conversations within, I've attempted to explore the development and working culture of individual studios, going on to focus on specific concerns of their work. Although this might lead to some frustrations because particular elements of particular projects have not been talked about, it is hoped that the discussions will lead to a more informed insight into particular parts of the process. This is about the work of making videogames as experienced by less visible professionals, covering a spread of platforms, genres and economies to shine a light on the breadth of the form. Thus, amid discussion of high-budget console development, you'll also find mobile-phone games, shareware titles and bespoke controller developments.

At the time of writing, the 'next-gen' development age that many of the interviewees refer to has just become a consumer reality. Microsoft, Sony and Nintendo have all released their newest hardware onto the market and the cultural, critical and sales battles have begun. This new hardware cycle brings with it as many extraordinary challenges as it does opportunities. On the high street and in the media, the battle is being fought by marketing and PR companies, but in the development trenches a different kind of struggle is taking place. The exorbitant pressures of next-generation development are a recurrent theme of many of our subjects. Studios and designers are dealing with the rising costs of production in a wide variety of ways. This book attempts to reveal how those pressures filter down to influencing practical creative decisions. In attempting to get 'Inside Game Design', we've tried to look not just at the creative skills and processes involved, but also at how it *feels* to make a game. After all, videogames are made by people.

Perhaps the most useful service this book offers is to question what 'game design' even means. For each individual studio, for each particular project, the balance of skills that add up to 'game design' are radically different. Game designers are project managers, artists, auteurs, business people, writers, philosophers, musicians, enthusiasts – almost always polymaths. This is the hidden industry of games design, often hidden away behind a lining of corporate publisher PR. These are some of the most inventive, creative, innovative artists working in any medium today, and represent a stunningly diverse collection of talent.

One can't help but feel that if these voices were heard a little more often, the media, the politicians, the parents and the uninitiated might feel a whole lot better about videogames.

IAIN SIMONS
February 2007

clockwise from top left
1 Chris Davie.
2 Bizarre Creations studio in Liverpool.
3 'It's like a still life' – the team are fastidious in their dedication to accuracy in recreating real-life city streets in *Project Gotham Racing*.
4 Martyn Chudley, MD of Bizarre Creations.
5 *Project Gotham Racing 3*, launch title for Xbox 360.

BIZARRE CREATIONS

www.bizarrecreations.com

LOCATION
Liverpool, UK

STAFF
150

KEY TITLES
Geometry Wars: Retro Evolved (2005)
Project Gotham Racing 3 (2005)
Project Gotham Racing 2 (2003)
Geometry Wars (2003)
Disney Treasure Planet (2002)
Project Gotham Racing (2001)
Metropolis Street Racer (2001)
Fur Fighters (2000)
Formula 1 '97 (1997)
Formula 1 (1996)

SELECTED AWARDS
Into the Pixel, PGR3, art selected for exhibition (2005)
MCV Industry Excellent, Development Team (2005)
BAFTA, Best Racing Game, PGR2 (2004)

BIZARRE CREATIONS IS ONE OF THE SUCCESS STORIES OF UK GAME design. Formed by Martyn Chudley, a veteran of the industry since 1994, it has built its recent reputation around the Xbox racing franchise *Project Gotham Racing* (*PGR*) and the unexpected success of Xbox Live Arcade title *Geometry Wars: Retro Evolved*, which has come to be the defining game of the platform.

Meeting Managing Director Martyn Chudley in Bizarre's custom-built studio in a discreet location on the outskirts of Liverpool is a disarming affair. Chudley is uncomfortable with PR hyperbole and is a candid interviewee when talking about his specialist subject – making games. This is something he takes extremely seriously. For all its success, the company remains relatively quiet, preferring to let its work speak for itself.

At the time of the interview, the studio was deep into development on both the next *PGR* title and its diversion into a new genre – an action first-person shooter (FPS) for SEGA called *The Club*.

Now you're into the fourth iteration of the *Project Gotham Racing* series, what for you are its defining characteristics?

Martyn Chudley What we're going for is an accessible simulation. In terms of working with Microsoft after *MSR* [*Metropolis Street Racer* – an earlier title developed by Bizarre for SEGA], we needed to make something that was more consumer-friendly – something that would showcase the new Xbox hardware as well as being a great title. So we were upping the poly counts, but we still had to make sure that the real cities were as close to reality as had ever been done, particularly in a racing game. We were trying to soften the game off, to make it a little more accessible to the players.

There's a huge commitment to realism in *PGR*, but there's obviously also a strong devotion to creating an exciting, engaging racing game. Is there a tension between the reality of a given city's streets and how exciting you need to make a track for the player?

MC That's an interesting question. The artists, particularly in the old days, wanted to make the setting pristine – every corner, every bollard, every lamppost had to be in exactly the right place. From a design perspective, we were going 'no, no, no! – we've got to make this more playable!' Always we would be trying to remove that bollard, shave a little from that corner – to make it better from a gameplay perspective. There's always been a compromise. We wanted to make sure that the city is completely recognizable. We saw so many games after *MSR* that made half-hearted attempts at that – 'there's the Eiffel Tower, so therefore this is Paris' – but didn't actually try to replicate the location. If you stood on any corner in our game, you would see exactly the buildings and landmarks that you would if you stood there in real life. That's a big thing for us, putting reality into the game. It's hugely gratifying for us to get comments like, 'I bought *PGR2* from the very shop in Edinburgh that's in the game.' Players can actually drive past, in the game, the very shop from which they bought the game in real life.

The fact is, it's very difficult to just make up a city. Cities have evolved over hundreds of years with thousands of different architects and styles, so to get one artist to sit there and fabricate a city from imagination that looks believable is an impossible task. Our approach is to let history do the work for us and remake what we see. It's far easier.

What proportion of your development time goes into that recreation?

MC Probably around two-thirds. It is down to a fine art now.

You've created an expectation that realism in the modelling is going to increase. Is this a burden for you now?

MC As a company, we have a core set of things that we think we're good at. We're quite feature-strong, so we like innovating in core areas. For example, in *PGR3* the cockpit mode was the key definer. We had huge arguments about it because I insisted that we *needed* to build these detailed cockpits – I felt they were really important. It's a small thing, but if you had proposed that idea in front of a design committee it would have been thrown out.

12 **Why did you feel the cockpits were so important?**

MC It's all part of the ownership you need to feel when you are playing of game. I wanted to give the player full ownership of the experience of driving these cars – all of which are well outside the range of what most people will ever drive. You don't get the sensation of just driving a different box around – you are actually driving a McLaren SLR or an Enzo. Every car is unique. And that goes down to the handling, the sound of the exhaust and the sound from within the cockpit – these were all things we individually recorded for each of the cars.

As a company, we really enjoy pushing the boundaries. I see design as being a cube, as opposed to a sphere. A game, I think, needs to have some edges to give it personality and make it stand out from the rest of the market. If you give that design to a committee, they'll round off all the corners and make it a sphere. It's OK, but it doesn't stick in anybody's throat. I'd prefer to have that edge, to have a load of people hating our game and a load of people adoring it, rather than a middling reception. I want to do something different. Sometimes it works; sometimes it doesn't.

In the *PGR3* credits, you have the singular credit of 'Game Vision'. That seems important: you're where the buck stops. How do you manage that on a creative studio level?

MC I'm the managing director, but I'm really the creative director. I sit with the guys and I say, 'here's the big picture', and we work on it together. I'm not a dictator – it's very much a team effort – but I will force things into the design if I think it's going to give us that edginess. That's at the outset, and then the production is driven by the teams. The time when I become thoroughly engrossed back into the production cycle is right near the end – the last three months or so. That's when I make the decisions about what's important and what isn't – what to focus on. That's what I feel my strengths are – being able to cherry-pick the things that are going to give us the greatest value at the end of the day. An artist may be working really hard on getting a specific statue looking just right, but for the player the statue is just a dot in the distance; it doesn't matter so much from the game perspective. My role is to take a step back from the detail and give a big-picture view.

Do you think that way of working is usual?

MC I genuinely have no idea how other studios do it.

You're culturally very much an independent developer, even though people often think you're owned by Microsoft. Do you think your operating culture is incompatible with being a publisher-owned company?

MC It probably is incompatible. I mean, I've just talked about making decisions that don't make sense. It can become very difficult to justify some decisions commercially. You go with the heart, rather than with the committee. It's almost incompatible with the industry; we're rare to be an independent of such a scale. However, we're having to change our approach, even within our independence. There are some things we do really well, and some things we do badly. We make great games, but we can't necessarily make great products. Great products are a combination of design, technology, art but also what the audience actually wants. We could very easily go off and make a great game that nobody wants to buy. That's where the publishers come in. They say, 'our research says that the consumers say they'd like this feature-set or these kinds of features', and that informs our approach. We're listening more and more to the publishers. It's really interesting and enlightening working closer with them on feature-sets.

So the publisher is very influential on feature-set development?

MC It's about presentation. People don't buy a game because it's a good game. They buy it so they can lose themselves in the experience, the dream of playing the game. When someone buys a game, they have an idea of what that game should be. They expect it to be the best, most playable, game they've ever seen – and obviously that's not the case. We need to make them want to pick up the product in the first place. We're on the back end of that process; people have already bought the game. The publisher is right there at the front.

Does the marketing process exist externally to the game you're making? How close are you to the marketers during development?

MC The presentational aspect is a big influence. For example, the games are all about kudos, showing off – respect and reward. We were always very British about that; very understated. Our game would say 'jolly well done. What a very nice slide you just executed around that corner!' In the future, what we'll do is call out the emotional content in the game a lot more explicitly. The game will say, 'Jesus! I have never seen anyone slide around a corner as well as you did just then. That was awesome!' It's really not just the content; it's how it is presented.

Chris Davie is the lead artist on *Project Gotham Racing*. He is closely involved in the practical production of all the city environments.

How do you select the cities for a *PGR* title?

Chris Davie The thing that really attracted us to New York was the bridges, as we hadn't seen these being raced over before. I worked on the Manhattan Bridge specifically. Once we've chosen a city, we map out a route zero for the track, and that's a real balance between the city and the potential track. There might be cities that would be really exciting to race around, but that doesn't mean they're spectacular to look at.

What research tools do you use?

CD Mainly the Internet; Google Earth is particularly useful. Before, we'd have to look at lots of disparate sources, so

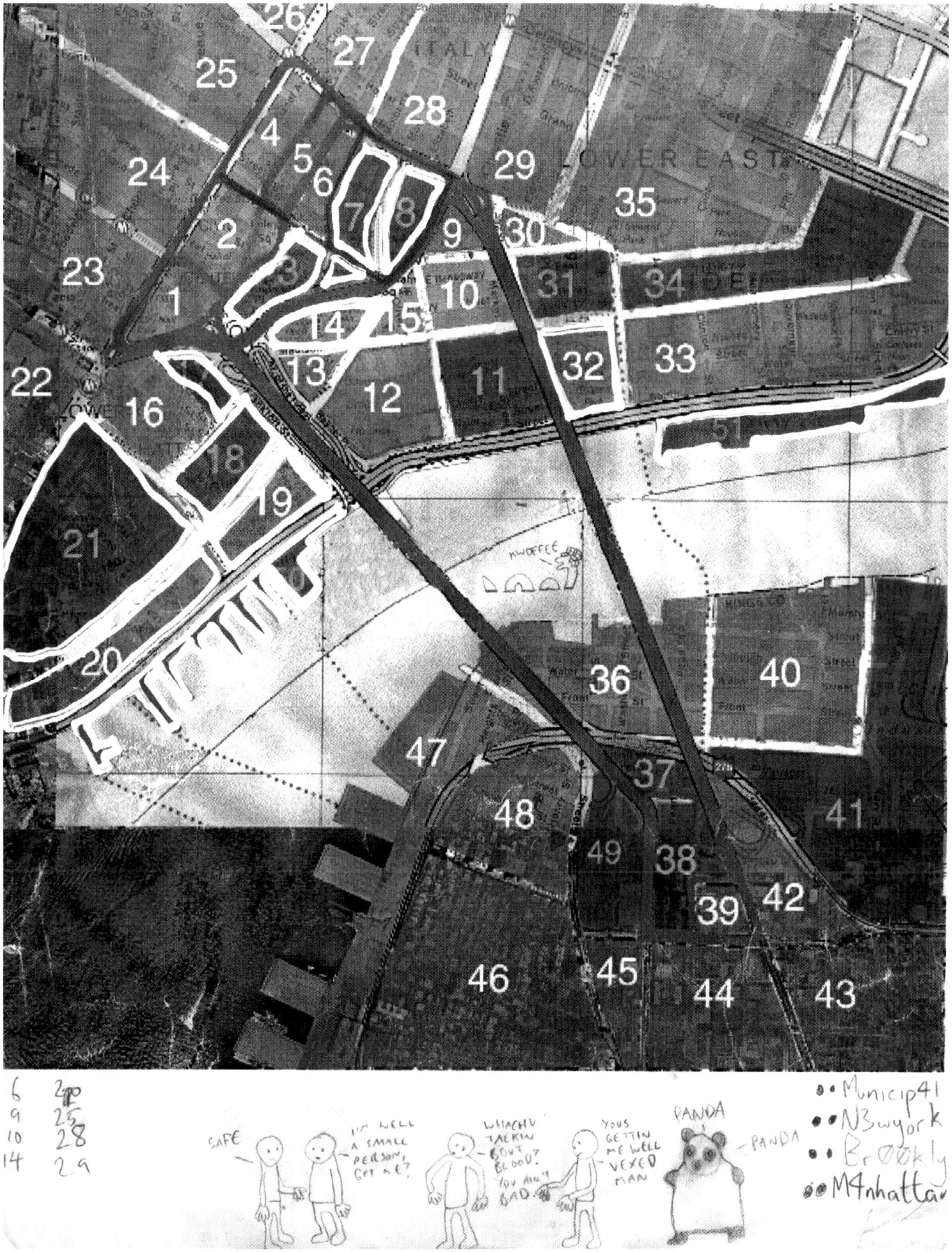
ITALY
LOWER EAST
6 9 10 14
25 28 29
SAFE
I'M WELL A SMALL PERSON, GET ME?
WHACHU TALKIN BOUT BLOOD?
YOU AIN'T BAD.
YOUS GETTIN ME WELL VEXED MAN
PANDA
PANDA
Municip41
N3wyork
BrØØkly
M4nhattan

below and opposite Models of the chosen cities are created from thousands of source photographs taken by the team. These are applied to the model geometries to create the texture maps used in the final game.

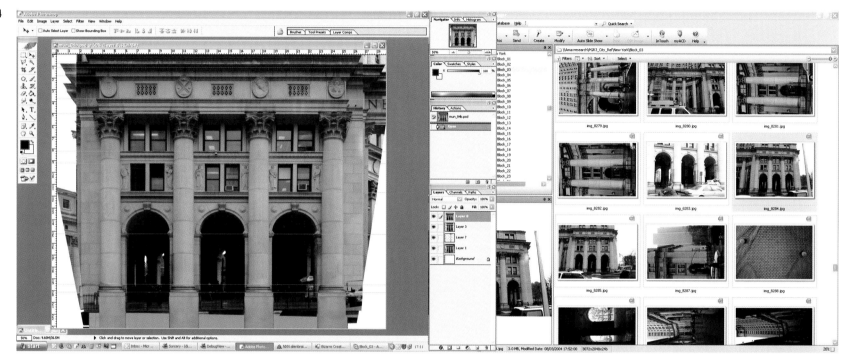

having things in one place is really handy. We don't use Google's assets, but it's fantastic as a research tool. Once we've chosen the route, we split the map up into blocks. This is the core planning stage – when we decide how many people will be needed, and how long it will take. Then we get out there. We usually start out as a skeleton team, with maybe three of us doing all the research. We walk down every one of those streets and take reference pictures of every single building.

It was quite tricky getting pictures of some of the buildings. One was a federal prison – it was legal to take pictures on one side of the road, but on the other it was illegal because you were onto US Marshal jurisdiction. You need to get permits for street photography for special cases like that. Once we have the reference material, we're pretty much ready. Then we start working on the physical models. That starts with making the footprint, often using satellite photo-

graphs. For New York we accessed orthographic projection maps from the public library, but they were quite out-of-date as the buildings change so often. We found a company that provided high-res satellite photography, which was what we used most for New York. All we do with this is cut around the basic footprint – once the city is divided up into blocks. Then you extrude upwards.

So the dimensions of the extruded buildings are based on the reference photography, not on actual plans?

CD It's all done by eye. First of all the buildings are sketched in as primitive blocks to make sure that the heights are all right relative to each other, and then we fill in the detail. As long as the vertical looks and feels right, that's what we're aiming for.

What sort of level of detail do you aim for in the modelling?

CD It's all case-by-case. For instance, for this municipal building we modelled the whole interior sightline you see through these arches, as you can see straight into it as the track approaches it head-on. If you drive towards it, that demands a higher level of model – especially as it's on a corner where the car would be going more slowly, so the player sees more. It's common sense, really. This took about six weeks – it was quite a detailed one. On average, it takes about four to five weeks. Block three demanded a lot of detail because you drive pretty much all around the block. If you drove down only one side and the rest was in the distance, it wouldn't need anything like the amount of modelling.

People sometimes suggest to me that it's not that creative, making textures like this rather than creating them originally.

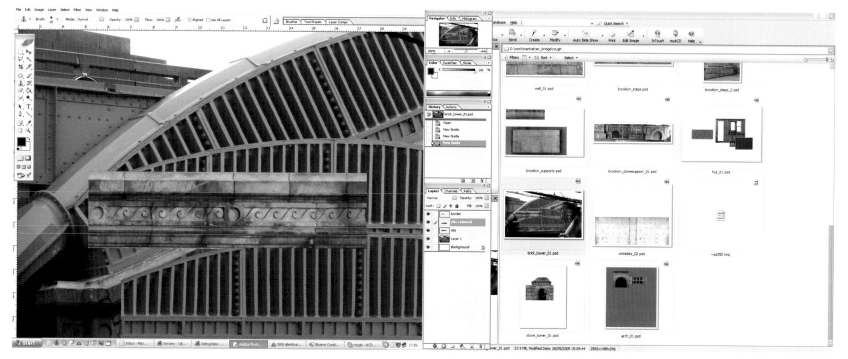

But then you look at what these little marks on the buildings actually mean – the little anomalies. For example, on one street there was a manhole cover that had road markings painted over it and the cover had been put down the wrong way, so the line was broken. These are the little stories that you get from this kind of process: years and years of use by real people. It's a still life.

this spread Modelled from sight rather than architectural plans, the level of precision needed for individual buildings is defined by their visibility to the player. This building falls directly in the view of the player as they approach a corner, thus the internal structure inside the arches needed to be created.

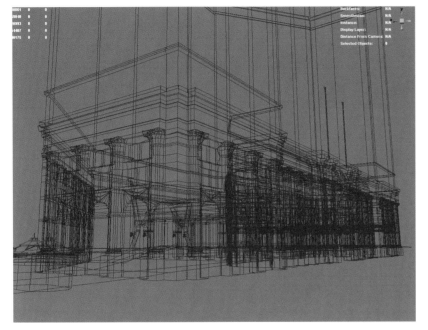

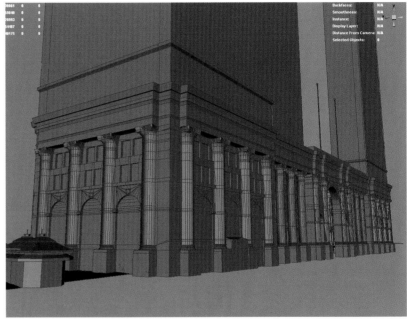

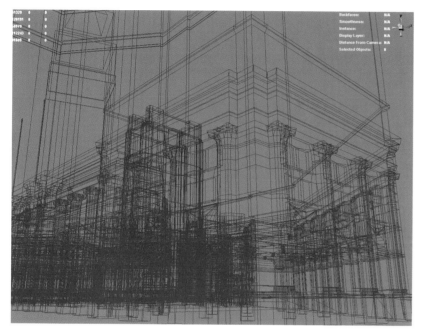

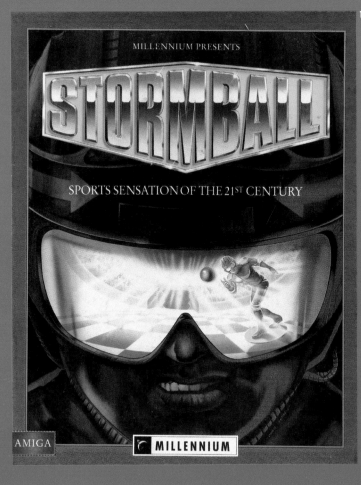

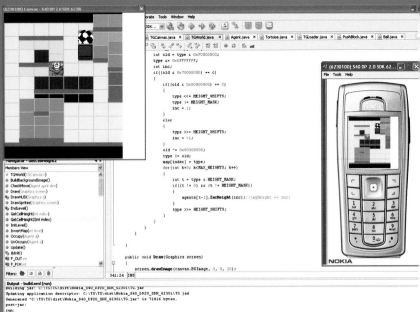

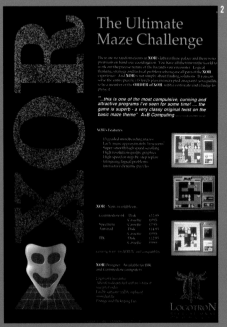

clockwise from top left
1 *StormBall* packshot.
2 A press advertisement for *XOR*,
one of Paul Carruthers' most
acclaimed games.
3 *Tortoise Garden* in development.
4 Carruthers' working studio.

PAUL
CARRUTHERS

www.monkeypoleclimb.com

LOCATION
Nottingham, UK

KEY TITLES
Monkey Pole Climb (2005)
Piece of Paper prototype (2005)
Rat Attack (2000)
Archipelagos 2000 (1999)
Batman Forever (1995)
Mortal Kombat (1993)
Terminator 2: The Arcade Game (1992)
Horror Zombies from the Crypt (1990)
Archipelagos (1989)
Quadralien (1988)
XOR (1987)

SELECTED AWARDS
International Mobile Gaming Awards, Best Gameplay,
　　Monkey Pole Climb (2005)

THE MODERN DEVELOPMENT STUDIO IS A TIGHTLY CONTROLLED, streamlined environment focused on getting the maximum possible productivity from a large team of people working under complex and demanding circumstances. It calls for an obsessive devotion to detail, a selfless commitment to meeting milestones and a deep grasp of multi-faceted project management by the studio director. Consequently, it makes few concessions to those who like to work in their underpants. 'That wasn't the only reason why I left', Paul Carruthers murmurs, 'but I'd be lying if I said it wasn't a major factor.'

Paul Carruthers has been in the videogames business for nearly two decades and has experienced game development in almost all of its forms. Until 2004, he was the studio producer on a multi-million-dollar MMORPG (Massively Multiplayer Online Role Playing Game) project. A pressured project with a large development team and a complicated set of intellectual property issues to manage, it was the antithesis of the kind of development Paul began his career in. As a teenager, Paul was a gifted violinist, but turned away from music to study pure mathematics at Warwick University. After a stint writing maths educational software at Loughborough University, in 1987 he and a partner founded their fledgling games company, Astral Software. They produced a series of highly successful titles including *XOR*, *Archipelagos* and the lesser-known *Horror Zombies from the Crypt* which, by Paul's own admission, was 'very poor'. The company continued with some success before Paul left creating original games to work as a coder for hire on console projects, which proved to be far more lucrative. He was particularly delighted with his royalty cheque from the Megadrive port of *Mortal Kombat*. 'It bought me my house!' he warmly recollects. Playing an executive role in the management of the studio delivering the MMORPG title, he found himself starved of the kind of creative freedom that attracted him to the industry in the first place. It was time for a change.

In 2004, Paul resigned and began to experiment in the world of mobile-phone game development. A much simpler and more open platform to code for, it reminded him of the kind of technological environment within which he used to work. Paul commenced working from home, free from the pressures of delivering a high-budget project, management and working in a team. This was much how he began his life as a freelancer, although this time, with a family present, the unsociable all-nighters and 'crunch' coding sessions were things of the past. What was the same was a far less stressful environment, which allowed him to work in his own way, wearing whatever he liked. The rewards of this initial risk came quickly. In 2006, Paul's first original mobile game, *Monkey Pole Climb*, won the Best Gameplay award at the first International Mobile Gaming Awards (IMGA), held at the 3GSM Conference in Barcelona. Encouraged by this success (and by the outsize cheque he was presented with as a prize), Paul continued to mine mobile as a platform for original development.

This interview took place as Paul was beginning work on a new mobile title, *Tortoise Garden* – which is discussed in the conversation. Optimistic about the future for mobile, and his place within it, he is an open and relaxed interviewee.

What kind of games do you make? How would you characterize them?

That's a difficult opener. There's been a very long time gap between my first bout of actually designing games and my latest one. I think there's a link though, which is that I feel that I always have to do new games. I don't get much pleasure from reinventing the wheel – making another platform game with a different theme.

I like to explore the area of the player having an effect on the environment, as opposed to the character, which is the more usual game type. I've only just realized that that's a theme, from games like *Archipelagos* and *Monkey Pole Climb*. There's no central character; the games are about environments changing and objects that are reacting to those environmental changes. Does that sound pompous? It's actually just some monkeys climbing up some poles… I think I try to provide a different angle, which may or may not work.

19

20

ARCHIPELAGOS

Atari ST
512K Ram
required
colour systems
only

When you talk about character, do you mean that both in the sense of a fictional character, but also in terms of player avatar?

As an avatar, mainly. As a designer I'm not really involved in game story. I've never found it a very interesting part of the job. As a player, I'm *kind* of interested, but ultimately, not really. I often find myself flipping through the cut-scenes to reach the actual game. I don't particularly enjoy games where the playability of the game is inextricably linked to the narrative, such as *Final Fantasy*, for example. I don't really care where the princess comes from. What I want to know is how the objects interact with each other to make an interesting place for me to play.

Presumably that's why you cite *Zelda* as one of your favourites?

And Mario. He's a plumber. End of story. That's plenty enough for me.

Because it wears its 'gameness' on its sleeve?

Zelda is a funny one for me: it is very story-driven, but when you've played a few *Zelda* games, the same things happen every time. But it doesn't get in the way of the gameplay. I see the games that I do as a kind of building block of proper games. They're sketches of games, but not fully formed.

Do you mean your mobile games?

I mean any of my games. As a designer I'm not particularly aiming for final game types; I'm just playing around with ideas of gameplay that sometimes work and sometimes don't. In an ideal world, I'd be able to take a game like *Archipelagos* or *Monkey Pole Climb* as a starting point for a second game and use those elements of gameplay that actually work to build a more publicly digestible game. One that might have a story and better characters.

I'm surprised by your comment 'sketches of games'. You mean the games that you've released are sketches of other, bigger games?

Yes. That's what I like about mobile games: the sketch *is* the final game. That's how the scope of them works, similar to the 8-bit-era games. You would look at those games now as part of a game, or an idea of a game, because it had a single idea. There was not much of a story or character; it was just a bit of a toy to play with. If you look at the history of games, often ideas from those games are harvested and put into bigger games. Your foundation elements have already been explored and proved from earlier, simpler games.

Can you give an example of that?

Take *Tomb Raider*. If you go back to its first iteration, it was built on elements of gameplay from an earlier Core game called *Rick Dangerous*. He was an Indiana Jones-type character, a 2D puzzle platform game. The first *Tomb Raider* uses elements of that, but in a 3D setting. You can follow the

Tomb Raider series through; some might say it hasn't built on that very much. I think part of the success of the first game is that it took elements of its gameplay from earlier games like *Rick Dangerous* or *Prince of Persia*.

It always reminds me of *Manic Miner*, with really unforgiving, pixel-perfect jumps. You wonder, particularly in terms of any discussion of character and gameplay, how it would play without Lara…

… or with *Rick Dangerous*. It's an action adventure game that uses puzzles a lot. It's a very good game, as was *Rick Dangerous*. The point is that that game, and earlier games before it, explored those puzzles – jumping over space, the way you walk onto a piece of ground and there's a short period of time before it crumbles away – they're classic elements of those kinds of games. My problem is that I think there are too few of those building blocks, those moments where someone makes a bit of a game and find it plays quite nicely. There's too much building on a single foundation.

Because of commercial pressures?

Partly that, but also laziness.

On whose part?

below *StormBall*, a futuristic sports game, used the same engine as *Archipelagos* but didn't enjoy the same success.

Designers, developers and publishers. It's very quick to make a game based on a previous game. It takes much more effort to make a new game. Take the example of the well-trodden world of action adventure games. Once you get beyond the Spectrum era, you have to make your own editors and tools for building the worlds and the puzzles. Your tools are built around the game style, so to add a different type of game style is an immensely hard job. It's far easier to bolt on a few ideas that take that genre slightly further in various directions. What interests me as a designer (and I'm not sure this is a particularly saleable trait) is the bare bones of games, the absolute irreducible keystones of a game. If you boil down all games, you'd find only a handful of core ideas.

How many?

Probably not more than ten. That would be an interesting exercise to do. There are clearly people who are coming up with new genres, but there are a lot of traditional game designers who are still basing all of their work on a handful of tried-and-tested methods.

Are you drawn to mobile as a platform because of that sketchability?

You can produce a game pretty quickly that can then be judged by a wider audience. It's not just about me having fun. Part of the pleasure lies in making an audience interested and excited by new possibilities.

Your first mobile game was *Monkey Pole Climb?*

Essentially yes. I was involved in other projects, some mini-games before that, but this was the first one that was mine.

How did it come about?

I was talking to some people about the mobile-phone industry, trying to decide what I might do next. This was an emerging market that was interesting and populated by a number of veteran programmers such as myself. Although a mobile is a simple machine and has to have fairly simple games, you find that people are playing games on their phones in very particular circumstances. Therefore, the games that they want to play have to be suitable for those circumstances. I find that very interesting. As a designer, you have to take on board a number of factors, such as the abilities of the hardware platform, and the age and type of people who are playing. Now, you also have to take into account the place, the time and the timespan in which people are playing.

Mobile games are typically played at a bus stop, so people can use only one hand. They might need to take a call partway through the game, or the bus might turn up – and those factors can't ruin the game. I find that fascinating. You have seemingly very constrictive rules.

I'm interested in how you begin to visualize these ideas.

Piece of Paper was initially an idea for a fly-swatting game. You press a single button to swat flies. I made a sequence of jumps from flies flying, to a piece of paper floating. That there might be some kind of game in keeping this paper floating…

… back to controlling the environment…

… yes, and the visual image of a piece of paper flying around just works for me. Adding up those elements, I felt there had to be a game in there.

So the idea of it being a piece of paper arrived at the same time as the mechanic. It's not a symbol, it's a piece of paper – it has physical properties that suggest more than just the imagery but the physics of how the game might work.

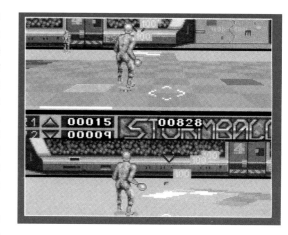

Absolutely. That came at once. I thought about doing a football keepy-uppy game, but that became a little too character-based. It didn't appeal to me as much as the piece of paper idea. It's a little more esoteric, a bit more outfield, and it's a lot clearer that the environment is influencing it. The football idea is interesting, but that's more about reactions. The piece of paper has more of a random element about it.

So you have the idea of controlling gusts of air to keep a piece of paper in the air?

You see a bit of paper bobbing about, and then you think about what kind of finger controls you can use on a mobile phone that are very simple, but the more you play the game, the more nuances you discover about how to drive this seemingly random piece of paper in a more controlled way. I saw this as a 2D game, with a load of pipes. There would be a single button to choose your pipe and then a single button to blow your air. I thought that would be a really good starting point for controlling the piece of paper. I explored that idea and made it more fun. Somewhere down the line I changed my thinking that the game would be better as a 3D game, and that was wrong.

this page

top *XOR* was one of Carruthers' most successful titles, being remade in tribute many times by amateur programmers.

bottom A still from *Quadralien*.

22

At the moment, I'm bypassing the whole pitch document/concept art route in favour of a much more indulgent way of prototyping. In a normal environment, you can't operate like that; it's too hard. There has to be a formal means of communication of what the title is, what it will look like, how it will play, what the USP will be, and so on, but it's just me. And because it's just me, it all happens in my head, over quite a long period before I even start.

What constitutes starting?

Starting is the time that I spend physically programming the game. I was involved in a commercial contract between *Monkey Pole Climb* and *Tortoise Garden,* but that was actually quite helpful as I had three months to mull over ideas and filter through to the best ones. What I have at the moment on *Tortoise Garden* isn't what I started with. I started with an idea of the basis of the game: there are two heights and a switch that switches between them and I can use that to produce puzzles.

So in the first instance, the game is switches and heights – not tortoises and gardens?

Yes. The point of the garden is that once you have an abstract idea for the game, you try to fit it into a visual context that will look nice and, more importantly, will help to convey to the player the ideas of how the various elements of the game work. Players can compare the images they see on the screen to their experiences in the real world and use that as a model for how the elements in the game might work. In terms of gameplay, the whole thing could just be blue and green boxes – but then the player would have to spend time learning what the blue and green boxes mean. However, if you show an object in the game as a football, you understand intrinsically that if you push this object, it will carry on moving, as opposed to an upturned flowerpot – if you push that, it will move and stay still. You understand that these are both objects you can stand on, but with the football you're

not quite sure what will happen if you stand on it. I had the basis of an idea of the core mechanic, but then took a while filtering through what might actually feel and play nice in the context of that gameplay.

And you do this in your head?

Yes. You imagine various pieces, objects and what role they might play, and therefore what interesting puzzle situations you might be able to construct from them. Sometimes they feel right; sometimes they don't. You can't tell until you prototype the ideas, but you can cut them down to the final ten in your head before you start.

How do you experience these rehearsals in your head? Is it a playthrough of an entire level, is it moments, or is it repeated elements until they feel right?

It would be nice if I could visualize the whole of the game, but I can't. I can visualize particular moves and the feelings of pleasure that you might get from solving puzzles – a little mental buzz that you get from figuring out how to do something. 'If I push this there, then that will drop, and that will allow me to progress' and so on. I'm looking for that buzz. I try to find it by going over and over in my head the kinds of things that the player might be doing.

Visually?

It's not a picture; it's more of a feeling. I felt it really strongly on *Monkey Pole Climb.* All you're controlling is the order of things. The pleasure is in controlling the order of them within a small amount of time.

When you're rehearsing these puzzles in your head, are you aware of the control interface too? Are you aware that you're imagining a mobile game and the physical control that makes it distinct from an Xbox title?

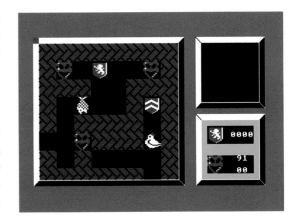

Absolutely – and I'm also aware of the programming implications. I'm always thinking about how easy or hard something is – that is, how expensive it is. That is what experience is all about; that is the importance of having done something for an enormous amount of time. You build up a feeling for something which includes a whole range of aspects: the ease, the expense and the graphical implications, as well as the gameplay. If you get a mix of those aspects that feels about right, then you know it's worth moving on to prototype it.

Creative people often report that a lot of their work takes place subconsciously, or late at night or early in the morning. Does this process take place wholly when you're awake?

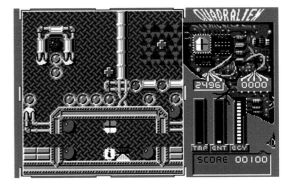

The best time for me is very early morning, around five o'clock. I'm conscious, but it's very dark. I'm very aware that I've been thinking about things in my sleep, and working out how things might play.

So this is quite a casual process – you'll be ready to start prototyping when you're ready. It's not a process you have complete control over?

There's no point starting until you're ready, when the feeling's right and you know there's enough there you can make a game from. This makes it really difficult if it's a job, because you have to make stuff to pay the bills.

It helps for me in my current iteration of jobs that I have other contracts. If I had to come up with a new idea every three months, that would be pretty hard. What will be easier for the future is that I've got the basis to build on.

With mobile work?

With game work. The basis of *Monkey Pole Climb* and *Tortoise Garden* (even though that's not finished yet) are ideas that I know I can build on, either for mobile or for handheld console. I can take a jump into a slightly bigger space having proved that the ideas actually work.

Does working on the commercial projects help with the personal projects you're working on imaginatively at the time, or do they distract from them?

They bring some money in, and they help me to program as well. They force me to do something that I wouldn't ordinarily do. Often I'll program around fairly complicated aspects for my own game, whereas for someone else's I'll plough through it and do it properly. That's just laziness, I think.

But it helps to inform the development of the next project. A lot of people with portfolio careers find working on multiple projects distracting. They would prefer to concentrate on one.

When I'm trying to produce very new stuff the point, I find, is that you can't be that creative all of the time. It's just not possible. However, I would like to be at the stage where I can do *Monkey Pole Climb 2*. I've got the two-player version of it in my head and I'd really like to make it. At the moment that isn't possible.

Do you have any anxieties that these ideas will disappear from your head if you don't capture them in some way?

Sometimes. There have been a few times in the early hours when I've had to go upstairs and write down the ideas I've had because I know if I fall asleep again, they'll just go.

What do you write?

Just a few words. Not an explanation, just something to help me remember.

What did you write for *Monkey Pole Climb*? 'Monkey pole climb'? That would cover it.

It wasn't a hint for the game; it was for the type of balloon. I went upstairs and wrote 'invertaballoon', and then in the morning I knew what it meant. In fact, in that instance I hadn't forgotten anyway. The idea was that a balloon turns a monkey over, or the next balloon has the opposite effect.

Having worked on a wide variety of projects, what kind of experiential lessons are you drawing on? 23

I'm trying to move away from the kinds of processes that are involved in a big project. They have to be closely controlled, from your tool chain to your team management. That means you can't make anything that goes too far beyond the current boundaries, because you can't afford to remake a complicated tool chain. You know how the objects and the environments have to be organized and there are various things that you just can't do.

What I'm enjoying at the moment is that I haven't got a tool chain – and very deliberately haven't – so I can try to do very new stuff. That isn't a long-term aim, but for the moment it's something that I'm really enjoying. If I was able to move these titles up and expand them to make bigger games for bigger consoles, then I would have to draw on that experience more.

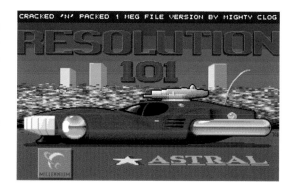

below Alpha mask for the Monkey
animation cycle from *Monkey
Pole Climb.*

24

What was your process with developing your award-winning mobile game, *Monkey Pole Climb*?

The first step was that I had to buy some books on Java, because I had no experience of it at all. I had experience of object-orientated languages and interpreted languages, so I was able to understand it fairly quickly. I found it complicated trying to learn what happens with all the graphical stuff, and how the phones are all different. I would have been better off choosing one phone and making the idea work on that one, and then tackling the fragmentation problem after that. It always helps me to learn something if I have a purpose for it. It was actually fairly quick; in about three weeks I had the basis of it up and operational. I made lots of errors, but you always do.

What was the basis of the game?

A prototype of the basic elements of the game. After that, I tuned the code to make it work faster and invented balloon types that would add something extra to the game – like the inverting one and the banana one. I then added things like dialogue boxes and pause windows. It was a matter of playing it and finding out if it plays well, or what I can do to improve it. The basis of the game is the order in which balloons pop out. I wanted to put time in to creating an algorithm that would make that feel right.

I had a problem at the start that the game was too random and it was too easy or too difficult. I tried various methods until I came up with one that was still random, but random in a way in which I could control how hard it was and how often it was throwing up bonuses. It feels odd if you get a whole string of bonuses in one period of time. I spent a lot of time on that, tweaking it and feeling through it. But then it was far too big, so I chipped it down.

What do you mean 'too big'?

The game went on too long. It was very samey. The point about phone games for me is that they're small chunks of gaming. The game is cheap, you play it intensely for a period of time and then you buy a new one.

Do you test the games on other people?

Not really.

Is that because the financial risks are so low, or because you trust your own judgment? *Monkey Pole Climb* won an award for its gameplay, but it wasn't focus-group tested.

No. I would test it more if I could.

What would you ask people when they were testing it?

Well, I tested it on family members, casually. I observed them, found out how easy it was for them to understand what the game is and how it works, and how fast they could pick up the functionality of different objects. It's a simple game, so generally people pick it up quickly.

Are you mindful of needing to test it on less game-literate people, particularly for the mobile and casual game market?

Absolutely. There is a whole different set of concerns. I'd like to build up a testing team.

Do you need to have things like the sound and visual design complete before you test the game? Presumably the main feedback you want is on the gameplay, rather than the sonic or visual elements?

It needs to be pretty much finished before you test it. You get all kinds of comments. People might say, 'I don't understand', and it's because of some *fundamental* part of the game. That implies that you should be testing earlier on, but I think my instincts should prevail until the point where it's nearly done. Testing is about balancing difficulty, making sure it can be understood.

One of the comments I got back on *XOR* was that it's fine once you understand how all the objects in the game work, but that's a long process, because it's quite abstract. There's a big entry barrier to people playing because the game starts

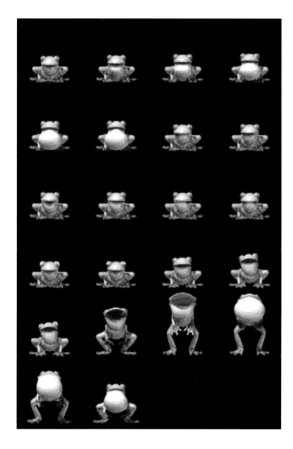

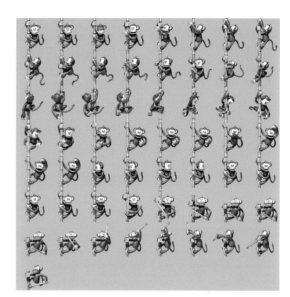

could be playing. It's my job to make sure those barriers aren't there.

When do you work?

I'm pretty ordered. I do office hours. It's very different to when I used to freelance when I was single. I suppose at that time I'd work afternoon/evening, but now I work morning and afternoon so I can spend time with my family. I start around 9.30 and finish around 6. I have a break for lunch if there are other people in the house; otherwise I go straight through. I tend not to break very much, especially if I'm really into the work.

Do you have to set yourself milestones in order to get anything done?

Very much. Because it's not funded.

Those milestones are entirely to do with money?

They're important for focusing your mind on what you're trying to achieve. It's very easy to drift off and spend a lot of time on something that's really not important. At the moment I don't have any proper deadlines, apart from the fact that if I'm not earning I'm getting poorer and poorer. Generally speaking though, if they were bigger projects, or paid projects, I would plan things out much better in terms of scheduling. At the moment it's great to have the freedom to do things as I want to. It's not for everyone, though!

and people look at it and wonder 'what the hell do I do now?' But that was from 1986 or something. At that time you made these games really quickly and bunged them out. It's a nice game that I have huge affection for, but it isn't right for this market now.

For mobile?

For any market, really. At that time people had more time and were more inclined to put effort into games. You'd buy a game and you'd make sure you understood how it worked. But now, if it's not fairly obvious straight away, people's interest moves on. There's a huge pile of other games that they

this spread Screenshots from the version of *Monkey Pole Climb* that won Best Gameplay at the 3GSM conference in Barcelona in 2005. Level 101 demonstrates an alarming spike in difficulty.

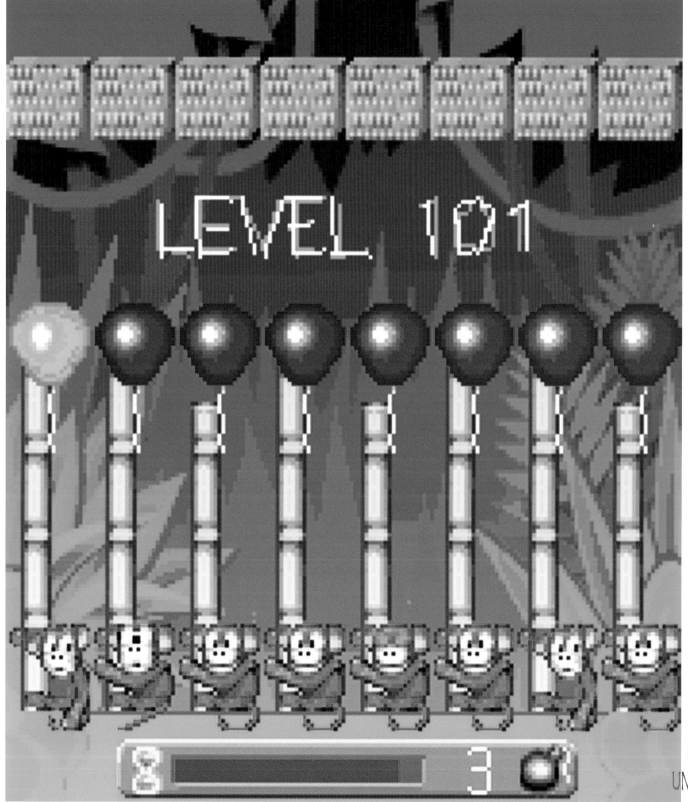

1

2

3

4

top to bottom
1 The Free Radical office.
2 Chad Ellis' (lead animator) desk.
3 Rob Yescombe's (screenwriter) desk.
4 Ellis and Yescombe.

FREE RADICAL DESIGN

www.frd.co.uk

LOCATION
Nottingham, UK

STAFF
150

KEY TITLES
Haze (2007)
TimeSplitters Future Perfect (2005)
Second Sight (2004)
TimeSplitters 2 (2002)
TimeSplitters (2000)

SELECTED AWARDS
Five BAFTA Nominations, *TimeSplitters 2* (2004)
DEVELOP Industry Excellence award, Best Independent
    Development (2003)
CTW Developer of the Year (2001)

FREE RADICAL DESIGN WILL ALWAYS BE AT LEAST PARTIALLY defined by the game its founders made *before* they were Free Radical Design. *Goldeneye 64*, which (Dr) Dave Doak, Steve Ellis, Karl Hilton and Graham Norgate worked on whilst at Rare, is largely recognized as one of the greatest first-person shooter games of all time – a constant fixture on the 'best games of all time' lists.

When the core team left to form Free Radical, the risks were high. With a team of just 18, the company was the only European studio to deliver its PS2 launch title on time, a bold high-energy first-person shooter called *TimeSplitters*. The extraordinary success of the title led to two sequels, both of which were critically acclaimed. Their first deviation from the *TS* franchise came in 2004 with a thoughtful psycho-thriller, *Second Sight* – a complex, narrative-driven thriller that unfortunately failed commercially but served as a clear indicator of the narrative ambitions of the studio. Free Radical obviously had aspirations to deliver new Intellectual Property that reached beyond the frenetic, colourful franchise of *TimeSplitters*.

In 2006 a new project was announced that was going to take the studio into completely new territory. The E3 show in LA was the platform at which *Haze*, their next-gen shooter with Ubisoft, was launched. The presentation of the game stood out as being something different. E3, for anyone who hasn't been, is a prohibitively manic tradeshow where games are launched to the industry, usually without any concession to restraint. In its presentation to the press, *Haze* appeared to be altogether a different kind of game.

The performance that launched the game was a short presentation by a representative of the 'Mantle' corporation, who evangelized its new defence technologies while infographic clichés and in-game footage played out before the audience. Several minutes of relatively by-the-book first-person shooter action played out, until in the very last few seconds the scenario suddenly turned and the audience was left feeling emotions they weren't used to experiencing in videogames. The sensation was unsettling; it was almost as if something considered, restrained and subtle had just taken place... But this is E3? How could that be?

Free Radical is exploring narrative, so much so that it now has a full-time screenwriter on staff. Rob Yescombe always liked games; he recalls as a child his father chiding him, 'son – you're shooting a load more people in a corridor again.' Rob, in a manner some parents might read as precocious, would reply 'But Dad. It's *why* I'm shooting them that's important.' The question of drama is one that runs through much of this discussion.

I met Rob at Free Radical, where we sat in the boardroom and talked about motivations for murder, writing and making videogames.

How did you find your way into the industry?

Rob Yescombe The games industry, even more than the movie industry, is an industry of enthusiasts. Everyone is here because they love games. Certainly that's true of Free Radical Design. My route in was a bit of a zigzag. For years I'd been doing script coverage and cable TV stuff. I had a few brushes with movies, and that was the direction I thought I wanted to go in. On a whim, for a change of pace, I wrote a sitcom that happened to get some good attention and was shortlisted for a prize. Meanwhile, Free Radical was looking for a screenwriter and was cautiously figuring out where to look. The problem is that everyone in the world thinks that they're a screenwriter or a novelist. Sure, large numbers of those people probably are, but if a company puts out an advertisement in the games press saying that it's looking for a writer, they'll get a hundred thousand replies under which maybe one decent script might be buried. So Free Radical advertised in very select areas, which is how I heard about the position. The weird thing about it is that the first thing I did when I left university was send a sample script to Free Radical, in the hope that they needed a writer. Back then, I didn't get a reply – the scumbags. Anyway, this time around they asked me for a two-page sample, and I sent them twenty. They asked me for a page of ideas and I sent them thirty. It's that enthusiasm that lubricates the birth canal to success.

29

30 **What kind of 'ideas' did they want you to send?**

RY At first it was a sample scene and a few game-design ideas under the loose 'war shooter' banner. They didn't need design ideas at all really, it was just a way of verifying that I actually played and understood games – they wanted a writer who could understand interactivity. If I have a reputation as a writer, it's for working very quickly. So I made a point to deliver more than they asked for, in half the time they'd given me. Previously, writing had been a group effort, with the designers, the animators and Dave Doak working together on the same script. And although their output had some great moments – I still rate *Second Sight* as having one of the best, and most intelligently handled, plot twists in gaming – because there wasn't any one person with enough time to write everything themselves, the end result was inconsistent, with the dialogue slipping in and out of character between cut-scenes and the in-game stuff. Furthermore, some of the guys were far too precious about their first idea for a scene, and wouldn't cut it down or cut it out. Me, I love the rewriting process because over the years I've grown to understand how much it can add to a script. The worst possible thing that can happen in any creative industry is having people who are absolutely fixed on one idea. It's very much the sign of an inexperienced writer. People looking to get into professional writing often say things like, 'I'm worried about sending out my idea because I'm scared it might get stolen'. I think, at the end of the day, you should be 1) glad if it gets stolen because it means it was a good idea, ergo you're good at what you do; 2) if you're not going to send out work you're never going to get spotted; and 3) if you've only got one good idea you're fucked anyway. Send it out. Never be precious. Just keep generating ideas and you'll be fine.

What happened after they made you official? Had they already set a story in place before you arrived?

RY Because I hadn't yet signed a NDA [non-disclosure agreement], they had to be pretty vague when I was doing a sample for them. When I first arrived, they had a very rough character arc, and some basic points they wanted the story to hit, but their atmospheric ideas were very clear indeed. The very first words out of their mouths were about *Apocalypse Now*. They wanted a modern war story, with genuine impact. That was their reference point. From there I started to think about what kind of narrative events would need to happen in order to evoke the kind of atmosphere that the audience experiences in that movie. Not to look at the politics of war, but the emotions of war. The thing that's horrible about war isn't really the fact that people are getting shot; it's *who* gets shot. If you don't care about the people dying then it matters less to us. That's the weird thing about action games – you'll shoot a hundred people in a level and not care about any of them. So, how do you get players to care about the people that they're killing? To a large extent, in a high-action first-person shooter that's almost impossible. People play those games largely because they want action. When they say they want an 'emotional experience' along with all that shooting, it's like saying you want a salad with your fried chicken meal. It's a token effort at a balanced diet, when what they really want is the chicken.

We're straddling a few ideals with *Haze*: we want to give the best possible fun, playable experience to those people who don't care about story and character – but at the same time provide enough story and character in the game to still make it rich enough for people with emotive tastes. We're in a strange place where we have to deliver something commercially successful, but at the same time we want to deliver something that people will talk about as having succeeded in artistic terms.

The atmosphere in *Apocalypse Now* that you were looking to recreate in *Haze*, is this really about referencing genre conventions?

RY I didn't want the script to be a series of sly nods to war movies, because it completely destroys any sense of immersion – the game becomes a quiz about pop culture. That said, clichés are useful things; using them sparingly is a quick way of letting people know what territory they're in if you're short on screen time. Find a way to use them *and* subvert them, and you're laughing.

In terms of 'referencing' *Apocalypse Now*, it was more about imagining the sensation of watching that movie in the cinema when it first came out. Trying to reimagine the impact it had on the heart and the senses for a non-military audience – almost none of whom had ever seen anything like that in their lives.

So your aim is to create a more complex emotional field of response within the player? Some responsibility?

RY We're not out to make something where the design forces you to feel something for these characters. In terms of emotional impact, we don't want to force the player to feel anything; we want them to just either feel it or not. Do you understand what I mean?

Kind of… Can you explain what *forcing* them to feel it would be?

RY Forcing them would be things like having a Game Over if you kill a civilian. You don't care about the civilian but you don't want to kill them because of the Game Over. That would be design trying to force you to 'feel' something.

So you're aiming for actual empathetic emotion, not gameplay system-based motivations?

RY Right. We don't want to instruct anyone in how and what to feel. The game is linear, so your physical path is forced, but we wanted to keep an element of emotional freedom. I figure your experience is more 'real' that way.

It was an honour to be entrusted with that kind of responsibility as a writer, because to a lot of people, writing is an invisible skill. They can't see or imagine the value in a professional writer until they experience the finished work first-hand with actors and special effects and so on. However, Free Radical has always been forward-thinking:

INSIDE GAME DESIGN

fairly few companies have a full-time screenwriter, doing everything from the pitch documents, to the outline, to the dialogue, to writing the manual; but it does ensure a consistency across the product.

As a writer, how has your process adapted for working in videogames?

RY For any script, the first thing I do is a beat-outline: point-by-point, the things that are going to happen, and in what order. Then I look at the events and see how I can create emotional peaks and troughs in them – how can I raise the stakes? Once I've done that, I have a skeleton that I can write around. My process is very intuitive. I tend to just sit down and smash it out, then rewrite and rewrite and rewrite until its right. The difficulty with games is that features and ideas can change in other departments on a daily, almost hourly basis, which can affect the script dramatically – dramatic situations might suddenly not make sense any more, because now the characters can fly, or whatever, so the script has to be able to follow that process. Adaptability is essential.

How collaborative is this process for you with the other departments?

RY Well – I've never been precious about my ideas. I always put out my work as quickly as possible for public evaluation. In the first instance, the Team Leads and I sit around with the beat-outline, and we talk about what we like and don't like. Once I've got a clear idea from them, I'll go away and churn out a first-draft screenplay. Then we'll sit down again, go through that in more detail and discuss what might cause ratings issues, or art issues and so on. Some writers hate rewrites, but I love every part of the process. That said, the most fun by far is when the penultimate draft is finished and I get to work with the animators and the actors. For me, they're the most important people of all because they're the folks who are going to perform that script.

My script discussions with the animators are much less formal. There's a lot of 'wouldn't it be cool if...' Those guys

---

He gets to his feet.

> MERINO
> Walk with me.

Merino carefully hoists Carpenter to his feet.

The two men walk slowly through the ward.

> MERINO
> We recovered as many of your people as we could. We are holding them at our village church. (beat) You and I were fortunate. (beat) Some did not survive the crash. (beat) People here say that I should not offer you my condolences, because of what your soldiers are doing to us.

Merino opens the door into the corridor beyond.

SCENE 29: INT. HOSPITAL CORRIDOR – CONTINUOUS.

> MERINO (cont'd)
> (beat) But I know that the world is more complicated than anger and resentment would have us believe.

Windows line one side of the wall. Outside, a FATHER walks with his 8-YEAR-OLD SON.

Merino sighs. It reminds him of something long past.

He opens the doorway at the end of the corridor.

SCENE 30: EXT. REBEL VILLAGE. FENCED PATHWAY – CONTINUOUS.

Carpenter looks up at the night sky. The air is clean. The sky is as clear as glass.

Merino's tone is sad.

(Handwritten annotations):

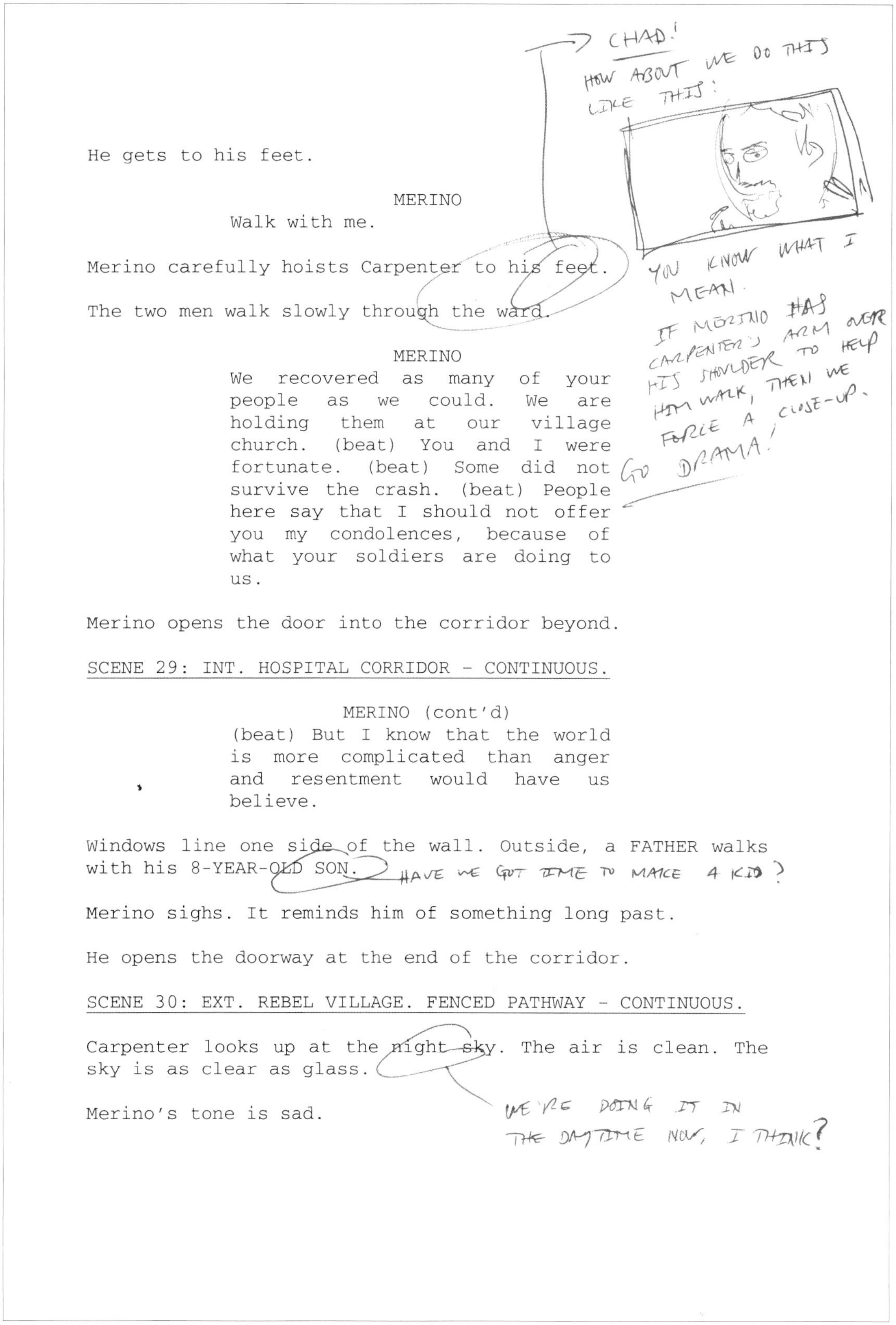

CHAD! HOW ABOUT WE DO THIS LIKE THIS:

YOU KNOW WHAT I MEAN.

IF MERINO HAS CARPENTER'S ARM OVER HIS SHOULDER TO HELP HIM WALK, THEN WE FORCE A CLOSE-UP. GO DRAMA!

HAVE WE GOT TIME TO MAKE A KID?

WE'RE DOING IT IN THE DAYTIME NOW, I THINK?

are endlessly creative, so it's a fair bet that their input will improve the script. Likewise, running the script past good actors is a quick way of finding any weak spots in dialogue. While I feel completely capable to do all these polishing stages alone, I figure that even if someone improves only one single line or event, it's worth it.

From there, I'll work up the next draft. Once there's a draft that Free Radical and the publisher are happy with, we get into the casting. For *Haze* we used actors I've known for a while – extremely capable guys. So many games have awful voice work, because a large number of actors don't take the medium seriously. It's still a pay-the-bills job for most of them, so I make sure we use really great actors who value their craft.

One of the things we did with *Haze* that comparatively few games do was make sure all the actors were in the studio at the same time. When they have someone to 'act off', their

performances really go up a level in a way that separate readings can't achieve.

Once we'd done the voice recording, Graham 'Beefburger' Norgate, the audio director, and I went away and made a 'radio play' of the story using test-score and sound effects. It's an incredibly useful way of communicating to everyone on the team what the game should *feel* like. It's also a great tool for the set-up guys, because they don't need to guess on dramatic timing because it's already there for them as the actors intended.

With the animation for *Haze*, we made a decision to use a lot of hand-animation. A number of games use motion-capture as a shortcut to animation. That's great for some action sequences, and we used it ourselves for parts of the in-game action, but hand-animation ensures a level of emotional detail and depth that motion-capture can't deliver.

For the motion-capture we *did* use in *Haze*, we brought in an actual ex-SAS operative and had him doing proper military movements for the Mantel Troopers. Those characters are professional soldiers, so the SAS guy was ideal. In contrast, for the rebels, we wanted someone totally untrained and unskilled to make sure the differences in military ability between the two sides really shone through – so, we used me. Believe me, it looks very authentic, because I had no idea what the hell I was doing.

You were talking earlier about how the writing can be affected by the rest of the teams? Can you give an example of that?

RY Well, the script was written before the levels were built, and the levels were still being built when we came to deciding what we wanted to do with the animations. So the animators and I would block out these amazing, elaborate scenes in a very physical way that from a dramatic point of view were perfect. But by the time we knew what we wanted to do, we found that the point in the level where the designers needed that particular scene to occur was either too small or the geometry wasn't appropriate in some way. For example, there's a scene where one of the characters is

tortured, which we imagined in a wide-open space next to a doorway that would lead into the next section. But when we looked at the actual level, the player was 50 feet underground, and the only way up was through a lift shaft. So, the scene had to be adapted to make sense with that environment. It was just another example of gameplay pulling rank over story – which is exactly as it should be.

So in terms of the in-game dialogue and speech strings, how do you relate to those areas in terms of supporting the narrative?

RY The gameplay doesn't really need to support the narrative as such, but it does need to support the reality of the world. The AI has to be on the money in order to believe you're in a human world.

That's shooting at you.

RY Yes. You have to have faith in your squad mates, and fear of your enemies. That's key to supporting the illusion that the scripted scenes create. If you've still got a believable world when the AI is running around doing its thing, then it's easier to maintain an emotional reality in the scripted narrative.

Do you feel limited by the genre conventions of videogames? This isn't intended as a criticism of shooting games, but the politics and depth of emotion within them are necessarily limited.

RY The thing is, everybody in the games industry wants a revolution, but the consumers don't. They still think they want better graphics or a more accessible control system. They want 'fun' over entertainment. Entertainment is a broad term – I can be 'entertained' by the news, because it interests me, but 'fun' implies something that makes you happy, and serious or political issues don't make anyone particularly happy. I think that's really the biggest difference in content between movies and TV versus games. If we're to be honest about it, the videogame industry is much more conservative than the film industry. Too many people want to play it safe.

Whether we like it or not, standard design games sell so many units that you've got to be pretty brave to try to step outside the usual sports-cars-guns mould.

It's the same with *Haze*. Although *Apocalypse Now* was the foundation, we inevitably had to pull back from that level of emotional extremity because our priority was, and always will be, playability. The game has to be fun. I'm the first to admit that as much as I value story and character, game design is the boss. What I mean is, in order to make a game palatable as entertainment there are certain boundaries that shouldn't be crossed.

For example, in one of the early drafts of the script there was a rape scene. I'd put it in there for dramatic purposes, but really there was no way it could sit right in interactive entertainment. If you're going to use something as negative as physical abuse in entertainment, it's our duty to show it in a truthful way, but as much as next-gen has allowed us to make the game world look more real, it just isn't real enough yet to cross that kind of boundary without it being in very bad taste. Although that could be seen as a limitation of the medium, it's important to keep in mind that there are other things that games are capable of that no other medium can compete with, which, personally, I think makes it a much more exciting field to be working in.

Chad Ellis, lead animator at the studio, joins us.

RY Chad was heavily involved in the casting process, which you might not necessarily expect, but the animators are actors themselves. They're the bodies of whichever actors we cast, so it's important to get their input.

Chad Ellis That was very well put. After the casting, we did the radio play. All our cut-scenes for *Haze* were in-game. With cinematic cut-scenes, it's more straightforward to block out those scenes in the conventional way, but for *Haze*, when you're working in first person and the player has camera

control, you don't have the normal conventions to fall back on – you can't cut away, and everything has to be animated in such a way that it can be viewed from all angles. The radio play gave us real useful shorthand for understanding the rhythm and the atmosphere of the piece as a whole.

The radio play is a fairly unique idea, isn't it?

CE It is. When we've done cut-scenes in previous games, we'd do the animation performances, edit the scenes, and then the sound was put on post. The actors would often dub over animations.

RY I think the other really useful thing about having the radio play is that instead of every single person on the project having to take a few hours out of their schedule to read the screenplay, they could sit and listen to it while they worked. So, everyone is on the same page without losing hundreds of man-hours.

Rob spoke earlier about the decision with *Haze* to hand-animate rather than rely on motion-capture.

CE There are certain things that motion-capture is really good for. Running around, deaths – deaths especially. They're much easier to make realistic with mo-cap. Although, of course, you can do a lot more extravagant deaths with traditional animation, so it's kind of a balance. As far as motion-captured performances go, I've yet to see cut-scenes that are mo-capped really give a powerful emotional performance.

RY The problem with motion-capture is that people get lazy because it looks, in a broad way, 'realistic'. But the attention to detail can't be there in the performance. With key-frame animation, every second has to be thought about equally.

CE More often than not you get a very generic performance with mo-cap.

This is a very different art style from previous Free Radical games. Are there any particular reference points for you as an animator?

CE For me, the main reference for this project is *Black Hawk Down*. It pretty much has all the elements we're using. Helicopters dropping down, the chaos of the war, the heroism but then the real horror that makes you think 'I don't want to be there.' That's what we're trying to get across in *Haze* so that was a key reference point for me. When we were doing the Ubisoft pitch I did a pre-visualization to show the two sides of the war in the game. I cut together a video showing first the excitement of war, the battle – it was a composite of the upbeat parts of *Black Hawk Down* and I put some really powerful music behind it, I think from *Backdraft* – and then, I cut together something slightly different from the same movie, but more gruesome and put some music behind it from *Band of Brothers* – which was very big and very emotional. So straight away you could see exactly the same movie, but put together in two different ways. That was a great way of getting the vision across.

How does the relationship with Rob work in day-to-day production?

CE Rob will come over and the animator will block out the scene based on what they agree on. Then we'll go over it together and make tweaks in the performance, 'this should be bigger, this should be smaller', because Rob knows what he's trying to get across in the story. And that works really well. This is the first time we've had a screenwriter here full-time who's actually written the story and who's working with me. It's really helpful in animating.

this spread Character concepts for
Haze detailing not just the look, but
playable features such as weaponry.

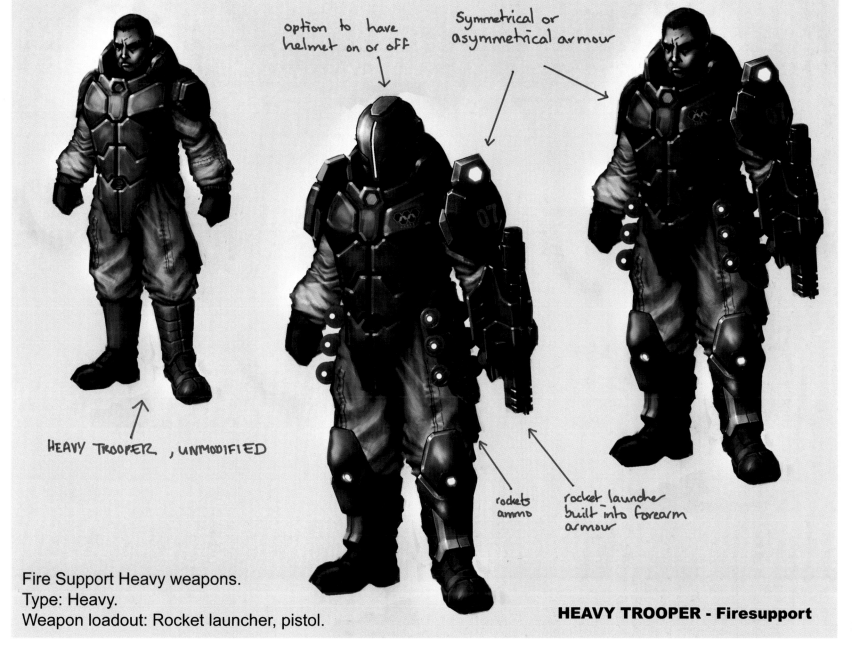

option to have
helmet on or off

Symmetrical or
asymmetrical armour

HEAVY TROOPER , UNMODIFIED

rockets
ammo

rocket launcher
built into forearm
armour

Fire Support Heavy weapons.
Type: Heavy.
Weapon loadout: Rocket launcher, pistol.

HEAVY TROOPER - Firesupport

Merino

36

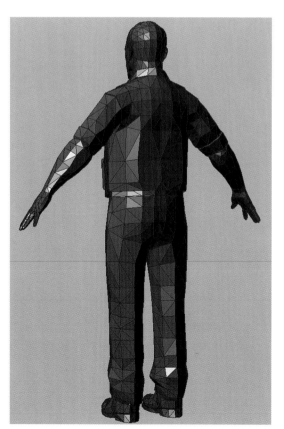

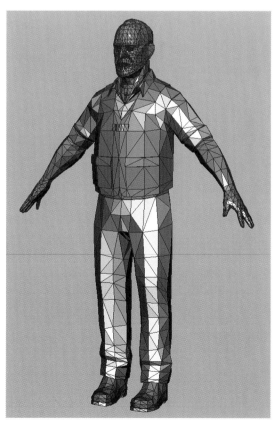

HAZE

1

3

2

PlayStation 2

PAL

B-BOY

TM

12+

www.pegi.info

FreeStyleGames

SONY

IMPERIAL HOUSE

4

5

FREESTYLEGAMES

www.freestylegames.com

LOCATION
Leamington Spa, UK

STAFF
40

KEY TITLE
B-Boy (2006)

LIKE A LOT OF THE INDEPENDENT STUDIOS FEATURED IN THIS book, FreeStyleGames was born of frustration; a group of like-minded people from other studios came together to explore different (and hopefully better) ways of making games. Founded in 2002 by a team of six developers, the studio began with a racing game project, which was attached to SEGA. Work on the project proceeded well, until the game was cancelled when a change in publisher priorities occurred following the merger between SEGA and Sammy. The future of the studio, which was already fragile in its reliance on a single project, looked in doubt.

Around that time, Sony, having just launched the PlayStation Portable device, were on the lookout for new Intellectual Properties to showcase the device and the culture it was trying to appeal to. Ever driving to align itself with unassailably hip sub-cultures, PlayStation was an obvious place for FreeStyle to which to pitch its next project. *B-Boy* was enthusiastically commissioned by Sony, initially as a PSP title. It was expanded onto PS2 as the studio launched into its first major development.

This interview took place just after *B-Boy* had shipped and FreeStyle had moved into their new studios in Leamington. Boxes were still being unpacked and signs being fixed on doors, and there was a tangible excitement around the place. Now some 40 members of staff populate the studio, which wears its brand and its culture with pride. Glass partitions frosted with the company logotype divide the space and there is a relaxed welcome about the place.

Chris Lee is both the public face and commercial director of the company. A games industry veteran, his previous work at Criterion represented almost the opposite of what he is doing now. Responsible for selling the extraordinarily successful middleware platform Renderware to studios around the world, he has a holistic view of games development studios that is relatively rare. His particular commercial responsibility tempers his answers with a hard edge; he's acutely aware when talking about culture and creativity that he's also addressing questions of product and brand. He answers both with candour.

Having emerged from a particularly corporate culture of the publisher-owned studio, he is now embracing independent development and the freedoms it brings with excitement – which is where the conversation begins.

I remember you being shocked at the GameCity event when a group of students told you that they didn't think there was any point in looking for work in the independent development sector; they felt they had to apply to large, publisher-owned developers. What do you think they imagine the independent sector is?

Well – bad news travels faster than good. Clearly over the last ten years there's been a spate of European studios struggling to survive. There are a lot of reasons for that; a lot of publishers went bust at once and the studios fell by the same sword. I also think that several indie studios just haven't been well managed. Commercial entities die if they're not commercially managed well. That's a reality. What we're left with now is a landscape in Europe of development studios that are really well managed and really talented, with more work than they can cope with. We've gone too far through the cull.

You get a different type of person who wants to work in an indie studio. It's not someone who wants to sit in their cubicle and just do their bit; it's someone who wants to put their mark on all of it. At FreeStyle we don't stipulate too heavily on roles. If you've got something you want to do, go ahead and do it. The profile of the people that we tend to get here is different to the kind of people you get in the big publishing studios. None of them are here for the cheque; they're here because they love what they're doing. It's easy to forget that we're in the entertainment industry. The pressure to deliver on deadlines and consolidate on franchises can make it easy to forget that we're supposed to be making things that are entertaining.

How do you find these people? Where do they come from?

We've recently hired visual effects people from the USA and the BBC, and an architect. It's great for us to get expertise

from outside, to get people to see how exciting the videogames industry is and see how their knowledge can make a difference. There are enough jaded people in the games industry – what's exciting for us is pulling new people in. People from outside the industry are often much more excited about it. For *B-Boy*, we hired a lot of people who had never worked in games before: a graffiti artist, four full-time B-boys, a DJ. These people had never worked in games before, but making games isn't rocket science. Making something that's entertaining – *that* can be difficult. We wanted to bring in people who understood what they were doing in wider terms.

You're in a great situation now where you're literally building a studio environment from scratch – studio arrangements, processes and cultures.

Yes. I'm fortunate in that in my previous role at Criterion selling in Renderware I got to visit a lot of both internal and indie studios around the world. That was great – five years watching the industry and figuring things out. When I saw FreeStyle start, I was really interested in what they were doing. The studio came about because these people felt that games weren't as innovative as they could be, they weren't being made as efficiently as they could be – and frankly, they weren't as much fun to make as they could be. We shouldn't be in this industry if we're not going to be innova-

tive and creative, and why should we turn up if we're not going to have any fun?

Were there any particular hallmarks that you noticed in studios around the world?

Japan's quite interesting. From what I've experienced, they have a few people leading the project and then a whole army of people making it – a lot like film, with producers and directors. The Western model is a lot more collaborative. The most exciting thing about the UK in particular is that we have real depth in all four areas: design, programming, art and production. Quite often you don't get that in a work-force, there are often more specialists.

this page Screenshots from the final game demonstrate the accuracy of the final animation, made possible through the investment in the motion-capture process.

43

this page Once motion-captured, the 3D data is used to build the in-game character models. *B-Boy* used a particularly large dataset in its pursuit of authenticity in the choreography.

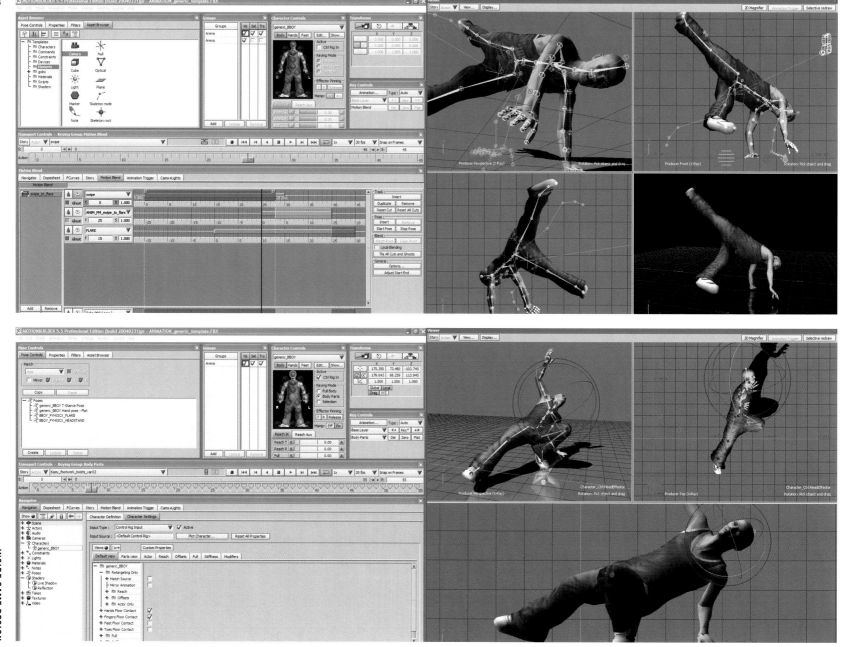

How helpful do you think it is to have a single person at the front – a Miyamoto figure? Could you see a similar situation emerging at FreeStyle with key individuals?

Not really. FreeStyle is the brand here. I mean, this industry is short of rock stars – we're short of people who can portray our industry really well in any environment. Where it works well, it's great – but it's a shame that a lot of the really talented people don't necessarily get the attention.

Lorne Lanning [see pages 142–49] made an interesting comment about auteur development simply not being in the shareholder interest at a corporate level – that the brand value shouldn't be contingent on an individual.

That's another reason for being in an independent studio. I think we need more characters who can draw people into the industry from outside. People want to be film stars, rock stars – but the games industry people are invisible.

B-Boy was particularly collaborative and tremendously ambitious in its attempt to capture and communicate the complexity of dance culture – whereas often games are simplified for greater audience accessibility.

We wanted to be totally authentic. When we initially took the idea of the game to Sony, they took it to a guy called DJ Hooch who is involved in the UK championships, and he was really sceptical. He didn't think it was possible to capture the precision of what the B-boys do and was suspicious of what he thought might be a cynical cash-in. This was a real problem: if you can't get the B-boy scene on board with this, then you can't get anyone on board. That was a huge part of the pre-production process for us – to get into the motion-capture studio with some of the best B-boys in the world and work out how to transfer their skills into a videogame. It's certainly the most motion-capture-intensive project I've seen; there was a huge investment of time and money to make it work. It was after about four or five months

of that prototyping that we went back to Hooch and he could see that what we were doing was credible.

Were the consultants dancers who gamed or gamers who danced? I'm interested to know how close the B-boys were to the development of the control system of their moves.

Really close. The people who played the game most in the early stages were the B-boys, absolutely. As we did more motion-capture work, the B-boys who weren't dancing would be in the green room playing controller tests of the game. There were other challenges, too. Originally we went for a more stylized visual appearance, but the feedback we got from the B-boy community was really negative. They felt it had to be as realistic as possible, which is what we went for in the end.

Did the control system go through a huge number of iterations?

Yes. One of our original ideas was to use the analogue stick on the PS2 controller to maintain your spin. So you would literally move it around in circles to keep the body moving. The B-boys really liked it, as it gave a real physical sense to the control. We wanted to keep that, but when we received the first development kits for the PSP, we realized that the analogue stick was just tiny. It's very difficult to get your thumb on it to make it spin like that, and we ended up breaking our first few PSP development kits trying to do it. We wanted the controls to be the same across PSP and PS2, so we ended up changing it. We were trying to find a balance between what we'd call the 'E3 audience', who need to see something happen when they press anything, and an audience who need and want this to feel as though they're still executing moves. We did about seven full revisions of the controls. It's a tough challenge. It's not a simple driving game – steer, accelerate and brake.

But it's not a flight simulator in its complexity…

It's as accurate as possible but without feeling like you're in a simulation. The easiest thing for us to do would have been to plug a dance mat in and go for it that way – but that wasn't something we were interested in.

What can we expect from FreeStyle in the future? What are you going to make?

We made a definite statement with *B-Boy*. We tried to show that videogames need to understand their audiences before you assume that the audience is ready to sit and plough through 20 hours of product. Games are consumed differently now – certainly by the mainstream. The audiences who want to sit in front of their big TV for 20 hours are there, but making more games for them doesn't necessarily take the industry forward.

Are you looking to collaborate with existing cultures, rather than make franchised exploitations of them?

You need to be influenced by what's culturally interesting, but you also need to collaborate. We're not in the licensing business: we make games.

this spread *B-Boy*'s concept art was particularly striking. Work by the artist, Chippy, was included in the esteemed 'Into the Pixel' show at E3 in 2006.

1

5

4

3

clockwise from top left
1 David Braben's desk (with dog).
2 David Walsh (Frontier's MD) and
Braben at their HQ in Cambridge.
3 Frontier have produced two titles
with Aardman Animation, including
*Wallace & Gromit : The Curse of the
Were-Rabbit.*
4 *Elite* packshot.
5 *Zarch* packshot.

FRONTIER DEVELOPMENTS

www.frontier.co.uk

LOCATION
Cambridge, UK

STAFF
135

KEY TITLES
The Outsider (tba)
Thrillville (2006)
Wallace & Gromit: Curse of the Were-Rabbit (2005)
Wallace & Gromit: Project Zoo (2003)
Rollercoaster Tycoon (2003)
Dog's Life (2003)
Frontier: First Encounters (1995)
Frontier: Elite II (1993)
Zarch (1987)
Elite (1984)

SELECTED AWARDS
AIAS Nomination, *Rollercoaster Tycoon 3* (2004)
BAFTA Nomination, Best Game, *V2000* (1998)

THERE ARE FEW INNOVATIONS THAT CAN BE PINPOINTED TO A specific release, a particular leap-forward moment by which further games will be defined as 'pre' or 'post'. David Braben was a Cambridge university undergraduate when the game he had written in his spare time with a student colleague, Ian Bell, was released. *Elite* was something different. In an early home-computer market awash with space-shooters that were wholly pleasurable, but equally simplistic in the motivations they offered the player, *Elite* entered the market as something utterly new. Its technical and design achievements read like a record of firsts: first 3D graphics on a home computer; first game to enable save-points; first game to feature completely open-ended mission structures.... The extraordinary critical and commercial success the game garnered won it a place forever in the story of the modern videogame.

Having made such an extraordinary impact with one of your first titles must leave a young programmer in a tricky and not entirely enviable position. Braben and Bell's relationship deteriorated and they split as work on *Frontier: Elite II* commenced. As Bell left the games industry entirely, Braben continued to develop within it, creating two sequels to *Elite* and a string of other critically acclaimed titles. He formed Frontier Developments in 1994 to house his work.

While not achieving the conspicuous commercial and cultural heights of Braben's first work, Frontier has continued to consistently produce some of the most interesting and reliably-excellent titles of the last decade (including the ahead-of-its-time pre-Nintendogs dog simulator for PlayStation). It has recently announced a new project, *The Outsider*, which will attempt to realize the promise of interactive movies in a way that has heretofore failed to materialize. Little has been seen in public of this conspiracy thriller, but its ambitions are extraordinary.

Braben himself is a generous interviewee, utterly candid but at pains to make sure he says *exactly* what he means, often offering qualifying statements to ensure that potential for misinterpretation is eradicated. In an interview taking place in Braben's office at Frontier, with his Dog nestled behind his desk, we began by reflecting on what motivated him to make videogames in the first place. This question, and his specific attempts to imagine possible answers, is central to his work. 49

Can you remember how you became involved in game design?

I'd been doing 3D work before I met Ian Bell. I made a shooting game called *Fighter*; it was very, very simple and very, very dull. It was just shooting spaceships. I played a lot of arcade games, but I found myself getting quite bored by their design mechanics. I was a little disappointed in that when I got quite good at the game – for instance, in *Defender* I found I could go round the lap faster and faster – it started to feel like a rather pointless exercise in hand-to-eye coordination. You don't get any real progress; you might get to see a new spaceship or something, but there's only so much progress to be offered. This was very frustrating to me. So when I met Ian Bell, we sat down and discussed how to make a game compelling.

You actually sat down and had that discussion, with a blank sheet of paper and a question at the top of it?

Yes. We sat down and brainstormed ideas. Interestingly, the first idea was a Space Navy game, based on hierarchies, but we rejected that because we figured people wouldn't like to be told what to do. And so we hit on trading, and both of us laughed and thought it would be dull. Who on earth would want to do trading?! And then when you think about it more, you realize that it isn't so dull, if you look at it motivationally, not least because it only takes up a small part of your time.

This shows the cynicism of game design to some extent, but one of your key considerations is 'what can we give to the player as progress?' – and that tends to turn into, 'how many of these lovely functions we've written can we keep back until later as a reward?' In *Elite* we wanted you to care about the meat of the game, which is flying around, being shot at and shooting other spaceships – but we were both totally against the concept of score. It's totally arbitrary. You just

this page
below left and centre One of the most influential videogames of all time, *Elite* assured Braben a permanent place in the history of interactive entertainment.

below right Frontier built on their experiences with the *Rollercoaster Tycoon* franchise to create an original I.P. *Thrillville* for Lucasarts.

50

challenge we have is to move the story into the game. That's why it's so difficult and exciting.

[A popular formula proposed by co-founder of Intel, Gordon E. Moore, states that the number of transistors on an integrated circuit for minimum cost doubles every 18 months.] Looking at how much processing power has increased, the odd thing is that we're using that almost totally to create better graphics, not to rethink how the games themselves are actually made.

How do you feel about the prevalent idea that photo-realism is a kind of shorthand for emotional engagement?

I totally reject that. I mean, look at *Bambi*: you just need to get people to care. There's a real problem in this current

stop looking at it. I remember seeing *Battlezone* in arcades and seeing scores in the millions, and I thought that you might as well cover up those three zeroes, what's the point? So we thought, well, why not money? The Thatcherite view, as Francis Spufford [*The Backroom Boys*, Spufford, 2004] put it. All you're doing is trading score for improvements to your ship, which makes you care about both the score and the achievement vastly more. The other thing I detested was the idea of multiple lives. Why three? If you're going to have more than one, why not have hundreds? A lot of this arbitrariness came from hugely successful games like *Space Invaders*, just because they had three lives. This became a strategy for making the player care about the combat. The real achievement is that success allows you to move forwards in the game. This made the battles more tactical – sometimes it's strategically better for you to run away rather than risk death. You'd never do that in a score-based game.

It was interesting, because *Elite* spawned a lot of copies and imitators, and by and large these didn't really understand the core mechanics at the heart of our game.

Yours was an explicitly cerebral approach to understanding the anatomy of the game, gathering its parts before you assembled it?

We wanted to make a game that *we* would care about. We were making it for ourselves.

But you took the time to understand and notate *why* you cared?

Yes. I'm a huge film fan. I love to deconstruct films structurally and that really informs my thinking about game design and gameplay.

One of the recurrent conversations I have with game designers and writers is about the problem with the word 'gameplay'. There is a non-specific, shared assumption concerning what it means.

It's a huge problem. The word 'game' is a problem for me. It sets in mind for older generations something trivial, not serious. We're doing a type of interactive entertainment, and that all of the words that have been tied to it have been destroyed by all these interactive movies that came out. I wish I'd spoken out more at the time. Back then I just thought, 'that's rubbish, and I'm not going to play it.' If I'd realized the damage they were doing... So I'm sticking to 'game' for now.

To be able to recreate the feeling you get in a really good thriller interactively – that could really be something. *Elite* really only touched on the interactive story elements. In fact, the producer of *Frontier*, Gary Penn, described *Grand Theft Auto* to me as '*Elite* in a city'.

One of the things we're doing with *The Outsider* is looking at why people play this kind of game. To make you care, you need to have an input into why you're doing these things within the game. You have to *care*. Structurally, we mustn't lose sight of what it is the player really enjoys doing – but it's almost separate why they care about it. The biggest

this page Frontier have worked on a
wide and eclectic series of titles. Their
collaboration with Aardman Animation
on the *Wallace & Gromit* games has
been particularly successful.

51

generation of hardware; I think people are losing their way. In previous generations, the ways the changes have manifested themselves most obviously have been graphically. Now, that's good – the graphical quality, the beauty, can help with the immersion of it – but that doesn't necessarily lead to good games. There's so much more available in terms of how you can elicit emotion. The graphics are a tool towards creating empathy, but not an end in and of themselves. Don't get me wrong; I can get nerdy. Real-time radiosity! Ambient occlusion! How can we do that? There's nothing wrong with that – it gives us gorgeous pictures for the front of the box – but it doesn't make the game. Particularly with fifth-generation games, as far as I can see, so far all of them have been fourth-generation games with next-generation graphics. You need to revisit the way in which you're making

the game to take advantage of this new technology. Nothing has yet.

Is *The Outsider* a response to a series of frustrations? A series of unrealized potentials that you are setting out to solve?

No. I wanted to do this game for a very long time. I care a lot about storytelling. To achieve genuine flexibility in a game would be fantastic – *Elite* had it, but that was because the world was relatively simple. The story behind the game is about media manipulation, which obviously gives you a lot of potential for storytelling techniques.

The story unfolds in a way that is logical, but the order in which it unfolds and how it unfolds is in the player's control. That's fascinating from a gameplay point of view. One of the

opportunities we have is to do more things; we can't just use this next-generation technology to only make better graphics. That would be such a waste.

People's experience of moving through game narrative in the past has been that of moving through a bifurcating tree – the hypertextual, choose-your-own-adventure experience. Are you saying that *The Outsider* isn't just that experience, but better disguised from the player?

This is a totally different paradigm. This isn't a slightly more bifurcating tree of options. What we're trying to do is create a story where lots of things happen essentially independent of each other. In moving through a game you're moving through a lot of different spaces. You're moving through different geographic spaces, different story spaces, and those

spaces are different for every character in the story, including the one the player is driving. Each of those components has their own links to other ones. But they're not necessarily links that the narrative travels along, they're links that information travels along. You can't pin the story down because you end up with a spider's web that is utterly unmanageable. So you look at it in terms of character motivation. If the player were to take any action here, it would immediately trigger a change in behaviour in the in-game character – if he knows about it. So there's a link, a flow of information. It's philosophically different – it's still branched, but it's branched in a different way. I'm not saying this is a completely done deal, but we're a long way down the line and what we have is already really exciting. As we're going more into fleshing out these stories in more detail, we're realizing more and more that it's working, that you can take some action in the game and the story will still work. It's a world of CCTV too, so there are all kinds of great ramifications. There are a lot of ways in which the story comes together. You just

can't have the narrative branching on everything the player can do. Otherwise there's so little that they can do. You end up telegraphing choices; if you have a hugely important story choice you end up having to draw odd amounts of attention to it to make sure the player notices. It's just impossible. There have been games when there has been branching, of course, but it's so expensive to do. Unless you take the *Dragon's Lair* approach where if you make a wrong choice you're just rewarded with a snippet of being eaten by a dragon. We're aiming high. It's our job to keep pushing game design forward to keep games popular. If where we are now is all games ever become, then that's really depressing. What we've got is an entertainment medium that is interactive. That's all we are. If we only achieve the level of interaction where we are today, then that's hugely depressing. But I refuse to believe it is like that. There are so many more ways we can interact – not just through ever more elaborate control systems, but through how we interact with the games on an emotional level.

this and following spreads
Concept artwork for work-in-progress
The Outsider.

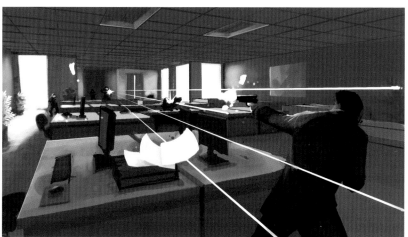

clockwise from bottom left
1 Gastronaut Studios – the way in.
2 Inside the studio.
3 Early concept art for *Small Arms*, showing the original title.

GASTRONAUT STUDIOS

www.gastronautstudios.com

LOCATION
Seattle, USA

STAFF
4

KEY TITLES
Small Arms (2006)
Fuzzee Fever (2004)

GASTRONAUT STUDIOS WAS FORMED THROUGH A COMBINATION of courage and recklessness. Jacob Van Wingen was a programmer (with his colleague Don Wurster) at an enterprise software company when he decided he'd had enough. He wanted to try his hand at games programming, although he'd never done it before.

Their first game, *Fuzzee Fever*, became a success on the original Xbox Live after creating a buzz on the indie demo scene. This led to the commissioning of *Small Arms,* which had just been released at the time of this interview.

Like Introversion (see pages 78–87), Gastronaut is a small indie studio factoring in a very real relationship between its design decisions and its resources. Although they operate in very different commercial spaces and create very different projects, the two studios share a casual audacity in the way they go about their business.

Jacob Van Wingen, the founder of the studio, spoke to me with Don Wurster, his co-director. They pick up the story just after *Small Arms* was commissioned.

Jacob Van Wingen I gave Don [Wurster] a call and asked him if he wanted to come up to Seattle and start a games company. *Small Arms* basically started as a series of conversations with me trying to convince him to move to Seattle.

When you left that original company, did you have a sense of what games you were going to make?

JVW I had a sense of what I wanted to make then, but I quickly realized it was way out of the scope of what I could do – strategy RPG [role-playing game]. Huge content games, very in-depth and we didn't have a huge amount of money. Gastronaut became a deliberate rescoping and examination of what kind of games a small studio can make profitably. Right now we're interested in small console games that involve lots of multi-player interactions.

So you started Gastronaut having never worked on a videogame? 59

JVW Yes. *Fuzzee Fever* was really intended just to be a port-folio piece. I took it to the indie games convention and it got quite a bit of attention. From that, a lot of people wanted to put it on this indie portal or other; it just came about. It's weird and great – the business became a business just because I got offers.

Was there an original high-level pitch for *Small Arms*?

Don Wurster We designed the game around the content we knew we could create. The pitch process really started when the 360 dev kits were just becoming available. We were talking to them right at the birth of the 360.

JVW Development didn't kick off properly until October 2005. That was when we brought on our second artist, which made us a full team of four. A lot of the engine was running and we had an example level running. We shipped 22 November 2006.

Our studio is one room. We aren't nine-to-five people. Our schedule varies, but it tends to be around 11 to 8. One of the big aspects of scoping our games is in working out how we can get the art done in the amount of time we have. We're interested in things like cartoony graphics. I grew up around NES [Nintendo Entertainment System] and SNES [Super Nintendo Entertainment System] and the sort of character design we have is very influenced by those. We can't chase a certain kind of photo-realism; we just can't afford it. It's much more sensible for us to set our own visual style.

How do you feel about Live Arcade as a place for games, and for your games in particular? What are the defining features of Live Arcade as a place for making games for you – over and above the commissioning and distribution model?

JVW Great pick-and-play games. You don't have to get up and put a disk in. You can be there playing a marathon

this page
The outhouse level: greyblock levels
(**top**) are made to test the playability
of designs before being developed into
fully rendered art (**bottom**).

60

Gears of War session, you can go to the dashboard, play *Small Arms* for five minutes, and then dive back into *Gears of War*. It's easy for those different kinds of content to co-exist in the one place.

DW The games that I think fit best are the ones that *belong* on a console. The ones that you just can't play on a PC because they need a controller, or they need the community infrastructure that comes with something like live arcade.

JVW The games that we make always have local multi-player. That's really important to us. Xbox Live is great, and it's one of the coolest features of *Small Arms* that you can play people over the Internet, but being able to play people who are sat on the couch next to you is a great feature too. That's something you can't do easily on PCs – it's one of the reasons we really need Xbox Live Arcade.

Were there any particularly challenging design issues in the production of *Small Arms?*

JVW The Moonbase level went through lots of revisions. Originally we had a list of levels in our design doc that we wanted to do. The original idea was that we'd do a level set on the Moon where the gravity affected the gameplay. We did a lot of work on this level with an elaborate and really interactive level with lifts and so on, but we scrapped it in testing as it just didn't play very well.

Our process goes like this: first we do sketches on the whiteboard of how it might play. Then we greyblock it – we take it into 3DS Max and draw all of the rough platforms, connect the scripts together and try playing it. So this is just a naked level with no art or textures. After we decide we like the way that it plays we do final models. Once that's OK we do textures. This one went through some remodelling until we decided we were all happy.

Do you test the levels outside of your core team?

this page
Early, and ultimately rejected,
Moonbase level design in test render
(**left**) and concept art (**right**) stages.

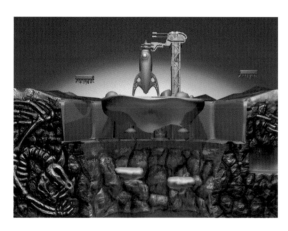

JVW We wish we could. We don't generally have the time. We occasionally bring in friends to play things, but it's usually just us. There was a time when we went to Microsoft's test labs, which was a real advantage of being so local to them. I really wish we could do more external testing ourselves. With *Fuzzee Fever* it was easier; I had a large apartment then and I'd just throw parties and set it up in a room for people to test.

There's one especially enigmatic feature in *Small Arms* that I've read about – the viral reward structure whereby you can get the reward only by playing online against other people who already have it, but it will spread only through six generations. I believe you called it 'Six Degrees of *Small Arms*'? That's a really interesting idea; can you tell me more about how it came about?

DW It's not as glamorous as I'd like it to be. I was at one of Microsoft's developer conferences when they were talking about achievements. One guy was rattling off a list of crazy things that no-one had implemented yet. One of the things he mentioned was viral achievements. I think Jake and I were talking about that driving home – what would that even be? What would the criteria be for using it? How can we get people to spread it? This is particularly important for us, because online multi-player was always going to be the focus of the game. Our goal with it was to get people to play online to get the achievement, but also something that people would talk about and have to look for.

We didn't know that we were going to be able to do it for a long time. Microsoft has rules about how achievements can be used. For instance, no-one can get an achievement based on someone else's gameplay. If you're playing a co-op game for instance, only the person who actually does it should get the achievement. We mentioned it to our producer who thought it was a cool idea but wasn't sure if we'd be able to do it. She called up a few months later telling us about a feature that MTV.com were doing about achievements; if we could get it through then we might end up being the lead in the article as it's such an innovative achievement. It was a perfect storm of a marketing opportunity and an idea we'd be incubating.

They put it through but insisted on some restrictions – that it would be zero gamerscore and that it would be unlimited in its spread. Originally, though, we only wanted it to be six degrees.

this page (from top)

1 Revised Moonbase level design,
reduced to basic collision
detection lines.

2 The greyblock of the Moonbase level.

3 Art and detection lines combined.

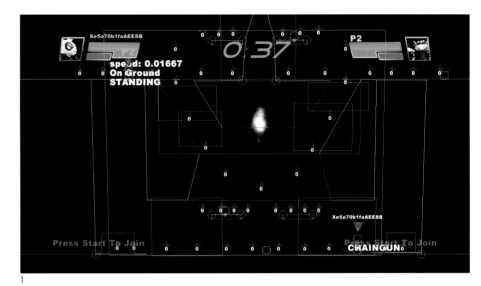

1

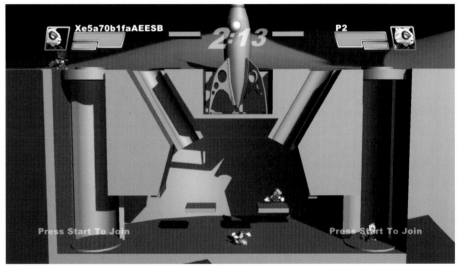

2

3

this page A sheet of head-concepts demonstrates the breadth of characters considered for *Small Arms*.

this spread *Small Arms* levels span a
wide variety of locations as this
concept art reveals. Players will be able
to download further levels and
characters using Xbox Live Arcade.

66

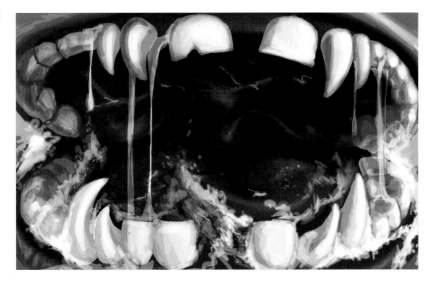

1

2

5

3

4

clockwise from top left
1 & 2 Harmonix keeps a particularly relaxed and creative working environment.
3 Lead designer Rob Kay.
4 Harmonix staff.
5 Bug-tracking the Harmonix way.

HARMONIX

www.harmonixmusic.com

LOCATION

Cambridge, MA, USA

STAFF

87

KEY TITLES

Guitar Hero II (2006)
Guitar Hero (2005)
EyeToy: AntiGrav (2004)
Amplitude (2003)
Frequency (2001)

SELECTED AWARDS

AIAS Finalist, Game of the Year, *Guitar Hero* (2006)
BAFTA Winner, Best Soundtrack, *Guitar Hero* (2006)
BAFTA Triple Nominee, *Amplitude* (2003)
AIAS Finalist, Outstanding Achievement in Sound Design, *Frequency* (2001)
BAFTA Winner, Best Lifestyle & Leisure Game, *Frequency* (2001)

HARMONIX MUSIC SYSTEMS HAS A MISSION. LOTS OF VIDEOGAME developers have them, but they are in most cases relatively non-specific intentions to make innovative, original and brilliant new videogames. Harmonix is rather more specific. MIT alumnus Alex Rigopulos (CEO) and Eran Egozy (CTO) didn't even start the company to make videogames; their aim was 'to create new ways for non-musicians to experience the unique joy that comes from making music.'

The studio developed music-led interactive attractions for a variety of theme parks before moving into game production with the critically acclaimed *Frequency* in 2001.

Global recognition hit with the release of *Guitar Hero* in 2005. This perfectly executed title made rock stars of anyone who wanted to step up to the PlayStation and grasp the guitar controller the game shipped with. The coverage and acclaim the title received were extraordinary, and it was adopted into that hallowed (and small) group of titles that even people who don't like videogames are allowed to like. Along with *Buzz* and *Singstar*, the videogame became a welcome addition to many a house party. It shared a lot with these titles, mainly the ability to bring about extraordinary transformations in whoever played it. The space in front of the television was transformed from being the place where you play the game to the place where you perform.

The design of *Guitar Hero* was led by emigrated Englishman Rob Kay, who discussed the experience of making the game over the phone.

*

Harmonix is a really interesting studio in that it has a particular mission and identity. How did you come to be sat where you are now?

I came over to Harmonix from the UK originally to work on the *EyeToy: AntiGrav* project, which was their one non-music game. The whole reason Harmonix was set up was to try to give the sensation and joy of making music to people who can't actually play musical instruments. Along the way, Sony said, 'we dig your innovative approach to gameplay, do you think you could rustle something up for the *EyeToy*?'

This was something of a gear change for Harmonix in that suddenly they had to find level designers, which they'd never had before. Luckily, I was a level designer in the UK looking for a new job, a new place to live, and a new challenge. I responded to the ad having played *Frequency* and *Amplitude* and loved them both. I came over for an interview and saw the prototype for *AntiGrav*. It showed a lot of the elements that were going to appear in the final game, but at that stage they were really just a collection of mini-games. So I started as a level designer on that game, then led the level design on *AntiGrav*. It was a research project really, an awesome and interesting project to be involved with. After that, we were approached by RedOctane to do *Guitar Hero*. I was lucky enough to get the design lead role on that, which was a nine-month project.

How did that project concept emerge?

RedOctane had been talking to Harmonix for a while. It was a rental company and then they made dance mats for *DDR* [*Dance Dance Revolution*]. It ended up selling a bundle of these dance mats and wanted to progress that side of its business. The company was interested in making a guitar game as they'd seen *Guitar Freaks*, which Konami had done. So they came to Harmonix with the request, 'will you make us a great guitar game for our new piece of guitar hardware?'

The peripheral led the project?

Yes. At that time, Konami hadn't released *Guitar Freaks* in the US, and I don't think RedOctane had any particularly grand ambitions other than needing a game. Relatively speaking, it was a pretty low-budget game – about a million dollars, which is pretty tiny as a game budget. We had a team that had just been freed up, as we'd just finished *AntiGrav*. This seemed like an awesome project. Everyone here was really psyched to work on a rock guitar game; it really fitted in with people's interests here. No-one had any notions

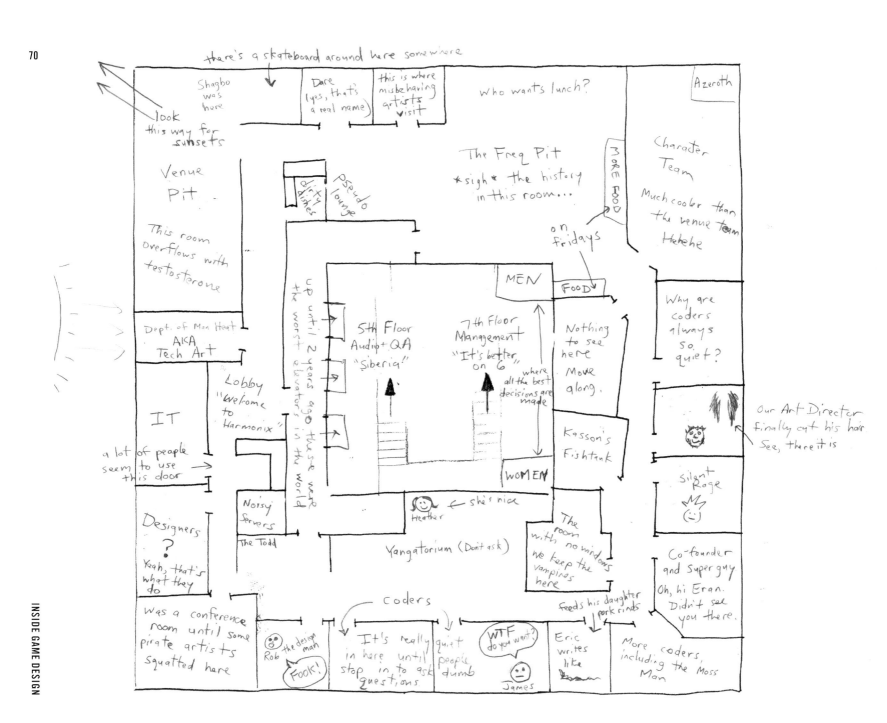

about it being a massive success; we all just thought it would be fun to do.

When RedOctane came to you with the request for a guitar game, how much of the detail of the project plan and the peripheral detail was already in place?

Basically, there were a couple of third-party guitars out on the market already for guitar freaks. When it began there was no hardware of our own as such, so we used those third-party ones. Our first port of call was to get the beat matching up and running using those. Our first visuals for that were like super-basic *Pong*-style graphics with white markers coming down the screen as the gems to match the guitar part [gem tracks/gem authoring: terminology used inside Harmonix to describe the beats on the tracks that the player has to hit. These are visually represented as little circles or gems within the game; e.g., on expert difficulty there would be one gem for every note within the song. To create easier levels, notes are removed – one gem for several notes]. It was pretty fun; the controller really was the kind of magic sauce for what we wanted to do. It's very difficult to make games attractive and accessible, and I'm sure that 90% of what draws people into *Guitar Hero* is that plastic guitar. They instantly say, 'I get it! I pretend to be a guitarist!'

Music is an easy shorthand for a lot of people.

It's a universal language. It makes it so much easier to make videogames reach out to more people.

Did you have a sense at that time of the visual stylings; the kind of cock-rock excesses you were going to be reaching for?

In our pre-production period, when we were doing the gameplay prototypes, we were also developing the art. Our art lead, Brian Lesser, was very involved in the East Coast rock scene; he'd been involved in making posters for gigs, so was heavily immersed in that kind of world. The design

really spawned naturally from people's interests – it wasn't as if they had to do a lot of research.

Were the key tracks in place when you started designing?

No, not at all. As we started designing the game we didn't know what the tracks were going to be. We had a wish list, but little control over it. As the project progressed, we gradually found out what the tracks were going to be. The music licensing process takes a long time, so we had to overshoot. We wanted 30 or 40 songs for the game and put a hundred on our wish list. As songs arrived, we needed to adapt the list according to what we could get – which were the easy songs, which were harder, which were popular, which were more niche. We had to constantly adapt the track list to balance those concerns as the licences flowed in.

Are you a musician?

Erm. I'm a drummer!

I think that counts.

I like to think so. The background of around half the people here is musical, but it's really important to have people that aren't too, to get that perspective in place on projects.

In our first prototype there was almost nothing on screen other than a simple 2D track. One of the things we learnt

from *Frequency* and *Amplitude* was that people don't necessarily relate to really abstract visuals; they don't always understand how they apply to them. From *Karaoke Revolution*, one of things we did was to put this whole musical creation idea into the context of a live performance. We aimed *KR* at people who had never played, and we decided to pull that approach over wholesale for *Guitar Hero*. In terms of the gameplay, there were really two main threads. One was the core beat-matching gameplay and making that as awesome as possible; making sure that moment-to-moment feedback was as good as it could be to create the sensation of really playing a guitar. The second thing was that as you'd be playing the guitar all the way through in this, we were going to need another layer of gameplay. That was where the idea for star power came from. That was there to provide a little more depth to the game – some replay value, some interest for people as they were playing beyond just hitting the notes. Also, a big part of rock is showmanship, and we wanted to find a way to explore that in the gameplay. The third problem was that we wanted to have tilt and a whammy bar, not so much as music inputs but as performance devices. We spent a lot of time discussing how that could be implemented, which ended up in the unified solution using star power.

How concurrent are these design strands, the controller development and the game development?

They were pretty much concurrent. We were pulling songs into the game pretty much constantly until ship. The licensing and recording process loop was going on all the way through production. It would be great if you could finish piece A of a project before moving on to piece B, but it rarely works like that. The way to solve it is by iteration: as the pieces begin to fall into place and you can see them responding to each other, you can evaluate and make design decisions as you go.

Presumably that forced you to revisit earlier song levels once the hardware features had all been finalized?

Yes. Most of the tracks went through some gem-track re-authoring, mostly for difficulty and authenticity issues.

What's the process for creating the gem tracks?

We have an authoring team who develop a feel for these tracks over time. It's about working with a track and being able to spot the key notes that will make you feel as if you're a brilliant musician. That first pass might take as little as a

day for a single song. We have a pretty large QA [Quality Assurance] team who can give them feedback on where it feels good or where particular difficulty spikes are. We also created some software into which you can feed a gem track; it gives you a difficulty rating back based on some rules that we've given it. By comparing those on a graph once the songs are in order, it becomes easier to make revisions to the set list – either by reauthoring or by moving songs around. So the initial process is relatively quick; for us the detail is all in the iteration.

And it was a nine-month cycle for the whole product?

From concept to ship for *Guitar Hero* was nine months, which is pretty quick. That's pretty much the way Harmonix

does things – the efficiency we've set up is fantastic. The team on *Guitar Hero* was around 20 to 25 people, peaking at 45. Around five programmers, one designer, one producer, one project lead, one lead artist, one lead audio and a lead QA. Behind them were the art and audio teams. The art team was easily the biggest team, split between track art, shell art for the menus, venue art and character art.

Having that process in place must have really accelerated *Guitar Hero II* production?

For sure. Everyone was excited and engaged by the project. We were also helped by the fact that we shipped towards the end of the PS2's lifespan, so we had engines in place that we knew worked and we knew the hardware.

It has been incredibly successful. In that initial prototype stage, was there any one thing specifically you could identify as being particularly strong?

It was all about immediacy. Someone could come to the game, be handed a plastic guitar and feel like a rock star within moments of playing. That ability to instantly feel like Hendrix or whoever was in place from day one. It was great to know from the outset that we were on to something that was clearly fun; we just had to build on it. We had a prototype of 'Back in Black', the AC/DC track, so that was the first song. It's really disappointing, as we never got the licence for it to be in the game. Hopefully for *Guitar Hero III*…

This sounds like a smooth process?

It really was. We're all used to games having to change their plans and agendas all the way through, and that wasn't an issue for us. The real challenges were in tuning the accessibility – so playtesting was key. It was really enlightening

seeing where people were crushed and where they were flying. Tuning that difficulty and creating that difficulty ramp was a lot of my responsibility.

The Quality Assurance process was focused mostly on the individual songs? The fundamental conceptual functions of the game were less of a problem?

Yes. The QA people were great at calling out all kinds of detailed problems with all of the songs – but one of the biggest things we have to watch is that people rapidly become good at the game with practice and that doesn't lead to the best feedback. We often try to bring friends and family into the QA process to make sure we get good information on the accessibility of it. From early on, it was clear that five buttons were going to be too much for a lot of people, so it was important that we could make the game work with just three buttons. We also realized we were going to need a tutorial, so we spent quite a while on that, introducing people to the game nice and gently.

We seem to be moving into a golden age of accessible gaming through peripherals right now. As a designer, are your thoughts led by peripheral potentials now?

I'm really lucky – since I started here I've worked on an *EyeToy* title and then *Guitar Hero*, so I've not been designing for a DualShock in years. The overriding enjoyment of that for me is being able to put games straight into non-gamers' hands and seeing them get it straight away. It's amazing how much of a barrier the standard joypad is. I think you only understand that fully when you take it away and put something more natural in its place. So I'm really excited about these potentials; it really helps us with our mission.

The other zeitgeist concept is user-generated content.

We talk about that a lot. The obvious goal is something like shared music composition, which as a goal is awesome. We'd love to find a way of doing that, people adding their own music into it. The technical challenges with that are huge, but it's definitely an exciting area. Then there's the aspect of customizing the look of the game with character creators and such.

Guitar Hero **is unusual in that it's an exciting game to watch people playing, and the in-game art and character animation are great for onlookers, but when you're playing you don't really see it as you're concentrating on your own performance. Like** *Buzz* **and** *Singstar* **and** *EyeToy*, **it casts the player as a performer. The game is less about the game and more about what it makes happen in the room.**

Absolutely, and you're doing it in natural ways people already understand – singing, playing guitar, doing a quiz… We put more art resources into the game than if it were just one person playing. The single player gets context from it, but really that's most beneficial for the onlookers. That performance aspect is a huge part of the game – people want to join it. With *Guitar Hero II* we spent a lot of time working out how other people could join in the fun.

this page The first prototype of the *Guitar Hero* beat-matching system. The basis of the game system can be clearly seen.

opposite page *Guitar Hero* character concept art. The game embraced all forms of rock guitarist clichés with abandon.

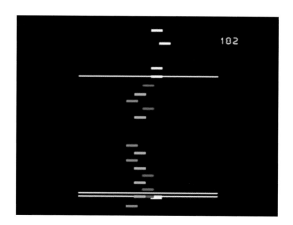

and RedOctane came to us with a controller. The guy with 'Game Designer' on his business card tends to be involved in the implementation of that mechanic, to the end of realizing that experience much more than setting the brief for the experience itself.

For anyone studying game design, the most important thing is getting experience in actually making things. Going through the process of creation is the most important thing; getting too hooked up on the ideas isn't going to help people learn what it really means to be a game designer at a development company.

It's great for us because people already understand the culture of this music, so we get a whole load of atmosphere for free. As designers we really only have to touch on something to get a whole load of sensation delivered. Like the star power feature – in a dry sense all we require you to do is tilt the controller up slightly. But what happens in the room is people end up jumping around and rocking out and playing on the stereotypes that they already have in their head.

Do you see yourselves beginning to get more creatively involved in the actual peripheral development?

We're trying to bring the hardware-and-software-designed-in-unison idea together more. That's not to say that we're going to move into peripheral design, as we're definitely not – we know what we're good at – but we're always going to want to be involved in that process.

Are there any important things about next-generation development for you? You're obviously not a visually led studio.

Sure. The graphical advances on 360 and PS3 are going to have only a limited effect on what we do. There are exciting advances in audio on those platforms for us, and the different control inputs are intriguing for us. The way in which Microsoft has implemented online console gaming is really

interesting to us, such as the ways in which we can connect people who are not in the same room. It's a really interesting leap with this generation: in many ways the consoles are very differentiated, so developers are going to have to think carefully about where they put their money. The thing for us is that now we're into the idea that custom controllers are the way forward in terms of engagement, we don't have a lot of the problems that other platform compatibilities have. We don't have to worry about how to make a PlayStation game work on a Wii.

On a personal level, can you talk about how ideas for games begin to form? How do they emerge?

I think there are two things. Most game ideas are about the experience rather than the mechanic. I think it's worth making a clear distinction between those two things. The game experience of *Guitar Hero* is being a 'Rock God' on stage, but the game mechanic is beat matching. When *Guitar Hero* was first talked about, it wasn't 'we're going to make an awesome beat-matching game'; it was 'we're going to make players feel like rock stars.' And I think the best ideas are ones that can be simply described in one line like that. To be honest, the game designer's role isn't usually to come up with that concept. For instance, with *Karaoke Revolution* Konami came to us with the experience idea,

1

2

4

3

clockwise from top left
1 Skilled, witty and shameless self-promoters, Introversion dress for the occasion to launch *Defcon* at the Ministry of Defence in the UK.
2 Chris Delay.
3 Times were hard. Introversion removed the middle-men by direct trading to the public.
4 Office play.

INTROVERSION

www.introversion.co.uk

LOCATION
Various, UK

STAFF
7

KEY TITLES
Subversion (tba)
Defcon (2006)
Darwinia (2005)
Uplink (2001)

SELECTED AWARDS
IGN, Game of the Year, Best Artistic Design, *Defcon* (2006)
Independent Game Festival Awards Winners, Technical Excellence,
   Innovation in Art & Seamus McNally Grand Prize, *Darwinia* (2006)

INTROVERSION STANDS FOR SOMETHING. IN ALMOST EVERY COMMUNICATION it puts out, its independence, its politics, its attitude is provocatively apparent. More than any other company of recent years, it has come to symbolize what the independent games culture could be. Through its singular commitment to creativity without compromise, Introversion has come to be the closest thing that videogames has to a guerrilla movement.

The most singular example of that so far has been Introversion's triumph at the 2006 Independent Games Festival with *Darwinia* and the company's subsequent acceptance speech. Mark Morris, one of the directors, gave a prescient summation of the Introversion mission: 'We didn't take money from publishers because we didn't want publishers fucking up our game.'

With success however, comes new challenges – in particular, how to maintain the company's culture as poverty recedes and the deals flow in.

Chris Delay has, to date, been the singular creative force driving the company. He spoke from his home, which is also his office. Living by the company's mantra, Introversion prides itself on being 'the last of the bedroom programmers'.

Could you tell me a little about the hallmarks of your games?

There isn't really a larger plan. We just think of things that we'd like, but also things we can practically get done. We're obviously constrained to some extent by the size of our team and the technology that we can develop. So we have to think of cunning ways around our limitations. We can't do anything that looks realistic, for instance, and that leads us down strange pathways where we come up with things like *Darwinia* and *Defcon*.

I don't think people would characterize Introversion games as small games. A lot of indies talk about the big opportunities as being things like Xbox Live Arcade and the opportunity to make back-to-basics simple arcade titles. Your games seem quite conceptually complex. They tend to be big ideas.

I agree. We're not really interested in making simple, casual games. When we embark on a project we have to be very excited about it and very interested in it. Part of that for us is definitely having a grander concept at the core of what we do.

Is that complexity present in the very first idea, in the very first high concept?

I think it is. The different game ideas have come in different ways. With *Uplink*, the whole concept of that game was very clear from the start. Right from the first thought I could see where the player would start and where they would end up, hacking into huge government mainframes. The whole concept and journey was there. With *Darwinia*, the process took a lot longer as that was a lot more technology-driven. We started with experiments using the landscape generator, and then trying to put loads of sprites on the screen, then we gradually figured out where the actual game might be. Eventually the higher plot and setting started to form. *Defcon* was more like *Uplink* in that everything was there right from the very start.

Defcon and Uplink – did you see those games as systems in the first instance?

They were a system, a visual idea and a setting. That's where it comes from. With *Uplink*, the visual idea was one of looking at a 3D view of the Internet, flying around down pipes and so on. That's nothing like how it ended up, but that was the original idea. With *Defcon*, the original idea was basically the end sequence from *Wargames*. Normally with us it's a visual idea like that.

But that was different with *Darwinia*? That project seems like the wild card in your work.

It is. But if you skip forward, the thing about *Darwinia* is that the first 18 months were just experimenting and trying

79

this spread *Darwinia* became
Introversion's breakthrough hit,
winning a string of awards and
considerable critical acclaim.

80

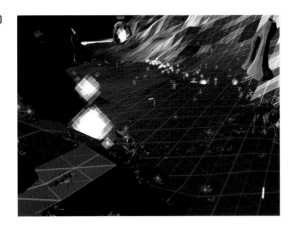

things out. Trying to figure out what might work technologically and what might work in terms of gameplay. There came a point 18 months in where we finally said, 'let's finish this. Let's stop experimenting and actually make a game now.' At that point we had a very clear concept of what that end product would be like. It's different in that we did spend all that time, but we did get there in the end.

We started with no real concept other than putting lots of sprites on the screen and having huge armies. It was a technological idea to get a hundred thousand guys marching around. It took a long time to arrive at the game.

Was it a challenge to try to render this vision of a large number of sprites in the first instance?

We knew it was possible, which was what triggered the whole project. We thought that there must be a really cool game somewhere that can use a hundred thousand sprites. You'd never see that number of things on screen usually. So we started working on a prototype just on that idea. It was blind faith that we'd stumble across a cool game eventually. What happened was that we downscaled that number. Every few months we'd look at it and think 'we've got nothing interesting here. This is just a technology demo.' We kept scaling it down and down until you ended up controlling just five guys in the finished game.

Is that a way in which you can afford to work any more?

We couldn't afford it then. It was a mistake. We didn't have any money. Eighteen months into the project, when we finally fixed what the idea was, it was still a really ambitious idea and took another year and a half to finish. The key difference is that we were more reckless then. We knew that we were going to run out of money long before the end of the project. We kept telling ourselves that we'd make it through somehow, and I guess we did. But we wouldn't want to do that again because it's insanity. You're taking out personal loans from the bank and borrowing money and you just can't do that.

We want to keep the ability to experiment, but lose the financial worry. So we're better off now than we were then. Then we only had *Uplink*, which had long stopped selling, so we were really short of money. Now we have three games which are selling continuously, so we're doing a lot better in that sense. *Darwinia* just didn't need to take that long. We experimented for too long and didn't lock it down soon enough. We could have finished that game and made it just as good if we'd wrapped it up earlier. We wasted a lot of time in the experimentation. Early on we had a lot of the elements of the finished game, but we didn't push forward with them. For example, moving the Darwinians around where you have the officer and they give out the orders herding the rest

– we had that idea in the first month, in the first prototype. We tried it and put it away and didn't come back to it for two years. If we'd been more focused I think we could have pushed forward and finished it a lot sooner.

Is that symptomatic of the size of the team?

There were two people on it. It's not really a team-size thing, just an experience thing. It was our second project and we didn't really know what we were doing.

I meant more in terms of being a small and distributed team. Is there less opportunity for rapid objective feedback?

I talk to the guys earlier now. With *Defcon* and *Subversion*, the others found out about the project a lot sooner than they used to. With *Darwinia*, I didn't show it to anyone at Introversion for nine months. They knew I was working on it, I just didn't show them.

What did you tell them you were doing?

I told them I was working on the next game. Simple as that.

Presumably they wanted to see it?

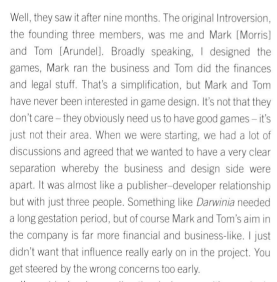

Well, they saw it after nine months. The original Introversion, the founding three members, was me and Mark [Morris] and Tom [Arundel]. Broadly speaking, I designed the games, Mark ran the business and Tom did the finances and legal stuff. That's a simplification, but Mark and Tom have never been interested in game design. It's not that they don't care – they obviously need us to have good games – it's just not their area. When we were starting, we had a lot of discussions and agreed that we wanted to have a very clear separation whereby the business and design side were apart. It was almost like a publisher–developer relationship but with just three people. Something like *Darwinia* needed a long gestation period, but of course Mark and Tom's aim in the company is far more financial and business-like. I just didn't want that influence really early on in the project. You get steered by the wrong concerns too early.

I'm not jealously guarding the design area; it's genuinely not their interest. It's changing now though with the whole company culture. We've always been pretty secretive in the past, with the public and each other. The first prototype of *Defcon* was completely secretly developed. Just a spare-time thing. But it's changing now; things like the *Subversion* blog are trying to share some of our work. Those first six months of a project are often the most interesting time because you're really rapidly developing all these new ideas, things are springing out of nowhere. Then you hit the middle

phase, which is always characterized by the end being completely out of sight and crushing doubt that the game is any good. And then it's crunch time to finish everything on schedule.

It really works. You are in a unique position compared to a lot of other developers in that they are not able to share that process for contractual reasons.

We don't have a publisher for *Subversion*. We can do what we like. I think that the people who are reading the blog at the moment are really just the hardcore Introversion fanbase, from what I can tell. We just want to share it. With *Darwinia* there were loads of great tech demos and stuff that no-one saw. It seems like such a shame.

As Introversion changes and grows, presumably things like that are going to become harder to do?

With some subjects – anything that involves another company. We're not just making *Subversion*, we're also working on other projects. But of course we're not going to compromise our contracts with those as information around them needs to be carefully controlled. We never said we were going to crack open everything, just *Subversion*. You're right in what you say; we're a bigger company with more

money coming through and more deals being made and we have to be careful.

Do you see that growing success as a threat to the Introversion culture you've already established?

Not really. For the first time now we have two teams. Before it's always been me developing the next game. Now there's me doing that and another team doing other things. It's not a threat, it's not a problem so long as the new project always goes ahead. Sometimes it has to be on hold while we get an external project done because obviously that might be generating more money – but as long as we keep making the next new game I think we'll be fine. It's funny – if you ask Introversion about its business ambitions, you'll get a different answer from each director. At the moment you're talking to the game design director. What I want is the stability to be able to make a new game without having to sell it before it's finished. Tom, for example, wants Porsches and Ferraris. At the core of the company there's this battle: now with four directors, each of us wants something slightly different. So we meet up every now and then and butt heads and argue and pull the company in different directions, and somehow it all manages to balance out on this even line. I think that's one of the reasons that Introversion works. If it had been three games developers running the company, it wouldn't.

this spread Heavily influenced by the final sequence of the eighties movie *Wargames*, Introversion's third game *Defcon* casts the player as a superpower in a nuclear war. *Defcon* bore the strapline 'Everybody Dies'.

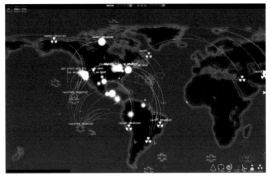
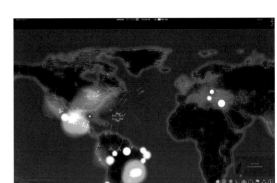

Can we talk about *Subversion*? I was really interested reading in your blog about the use of procedural content as a strategy for keeping budgets down.

It's a phenomenally economical way to generate huge amounts of content. At the moment, I'm working on procedural cityscapes, generating backstreets and main streets and squares. I don't need to worry about any of the detail; it's just generated by tweaking this envelope. Even if we could afford the artists, this code can generate something like this in far more complexity and detail than can be done by anyone. You can't generate things this size manually.

Do you think it's a lost art? Since Braben and Bell squashed entire galaxies into a BBC Micro?

I think it comes down to the industry's obsession with photo-realism. You can use procedural content for that, but it's not really what it's for. Over the years, companies have been focusing increasingly on photo-realism, and they end up modelling more and more by hand. The space available isn't a problem any more; if you have the time to spend, you can make the art. But if someone wanted to model a city for a game it would probably never occur to them to procedurally generate it. They'd probably just start drawing roads and placing streetlights and stuff. By the end, you'd have this huge cityscape that can be explored and everything in it was built by hand. So it takes years.

So is procedural content driving your design because of commercial concerns?

It's for a mixture of reasons. We've been asked before if we'd rather have a different kind of graphic look – does *Darwinia* look like it does because we had no money? We can't do realistic stuff, so we do stylistic stuff. But that doesn't mean that we can't make our stylistic stuff look great. The current project, *Subversion*, isn't technology-driven like *Darwinia* was. It's a real game-design concept. It'll benefit hugely from having these vast cities. Now, I'm not able to go and model a city in 3DS Max. I don't know how to, for a start, and even if I did I wouldn't have the time. But I can write algorithms that will do it for me. Once you get your head around these theories they really become your friend.

How are you going to make a city? Well, you zoom all the way in and work out what defines a road, then what makes a road divide into two. You make very simple local rules and run them over the whole area and these amazing things form. No-one designs cities from a high level – it's very rare. At a local level, cities all evolve naturally and they form these patterns. This is about understanding those patterns. *Darwinia* was supposed to be completely procedural, but we couldn't make it work. We weren't clever enough then, so we ended up making map editors and there were only ten levels in the game as a consequence, rather than it generating a new level for you every time you played.

this spread Extracts from Delay's *Uplink* development bible. This document contains all his notes and design ideas for the game.

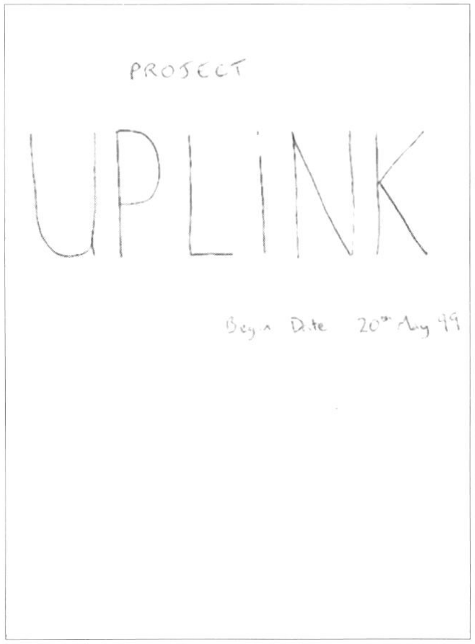
PROJECT
UPLiNK
Begin Date 20th Aug 99

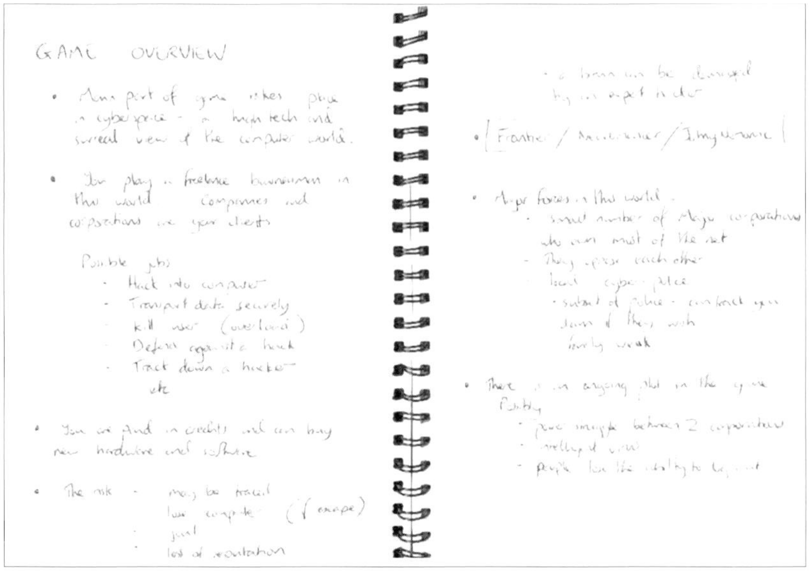
GAME OVERVIEW
• Main part of game takes place in cyberspace - a high tech and surreal view of the computer world.
• You play a freelance businessman in this world. Companies and corporations are your clients
Possible jobs
- Hack into computer
- Transport data securely
- Kill user (overload)
- Defend against a hack
- Track down a hacker
etc
• You are paid in credits and can buy new hardware and software
• The risk - may be traced
lose computer
lost of reputation
• Major forces in the world.
- Small number of Major corporations who own most of the net
- They oppose each other
• There is an ongoing plot in the game
- power struggle between 2 corporations
- people lose the ability to

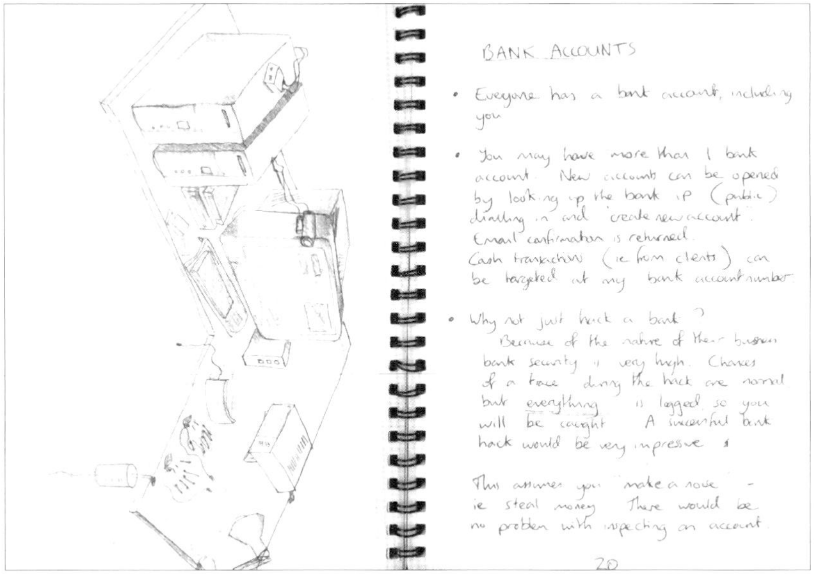
BANK ACCOUNTS
• Everyone has a bank account, including you
• You may have more than 1 bank account. New accounts can be opened by looking up the bank IP (public) dialling in and 'create new account'. Email confirmation is returned.
Cash transactions (ie from clients) can be targeted at any bank account number
• Why not just hack a bank ?
Because of the nature of their business bank security is very high. Chances of a trace during the hack are normal but everything is logged so you will be caught. A successful bank hack would be very impressive
This assumes you make a move - ie steal money. There would be no problem with inspecting an account.
20

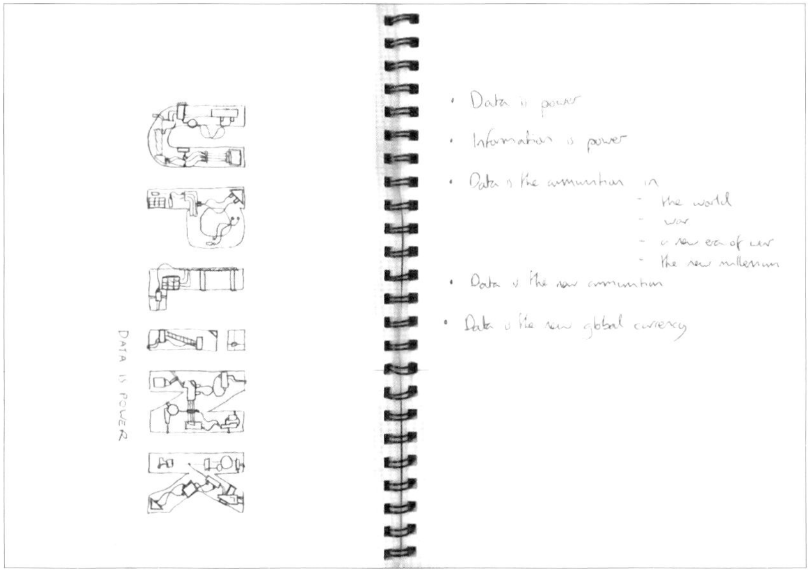
DATA IS POWER
• Data is power
• Information is power
• Data is the ammunition in
- the world
- war
- the new millennium
• Data is the new ammunition
• Data is the new global currency

following spread Procedural city generation for Introversion's new project *Subversion*.

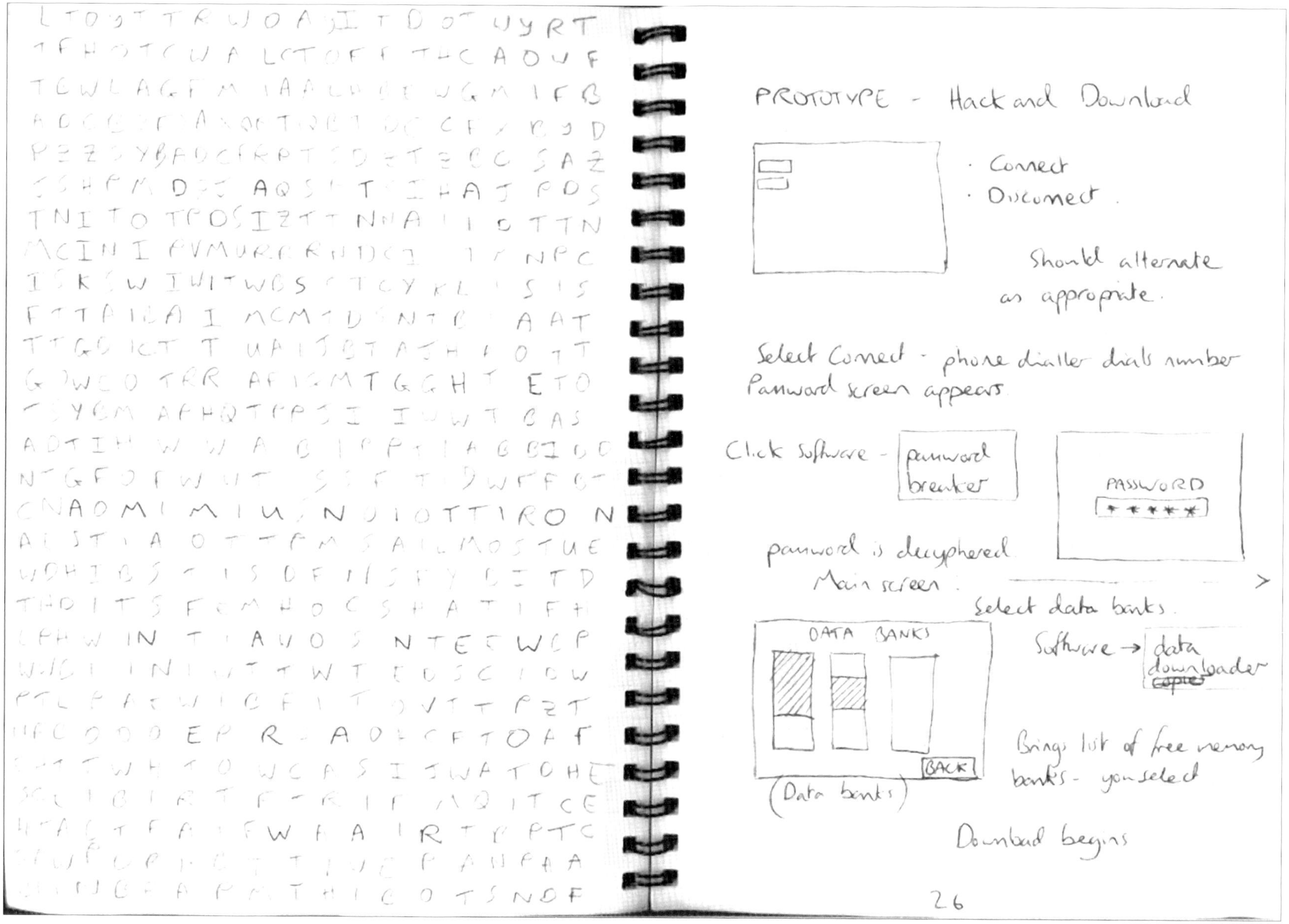

PROTOTYPE - Hack and Download

· Connect
· Disconnect.

Should alternate as appropriate.

Select Connect - phone dialler dials number
Password screen appears.

Click Software - password breaker

PASSWORD
[* * * * *]

password is deciphered.
Main screen.

Select data banks.

DATA BANKS

[BACK]

(Data banks)

Software → data downloader ~~copier~~

Brings list of free memory banks - you select

Download begins

26

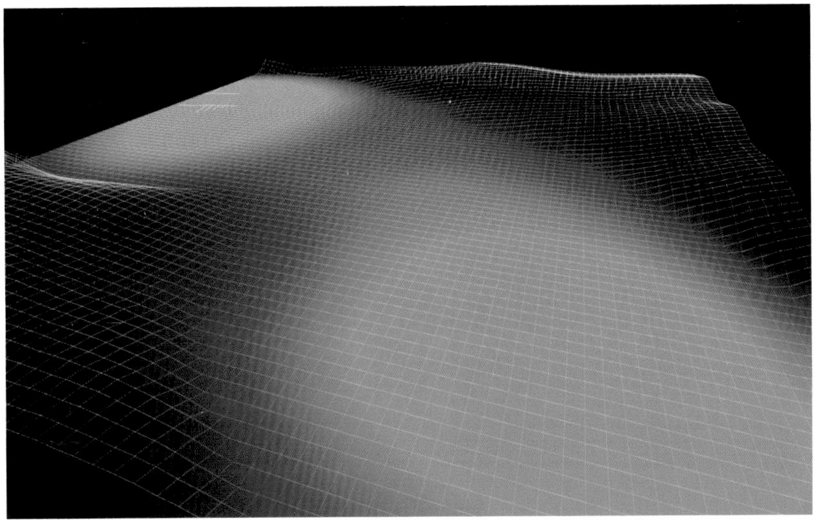

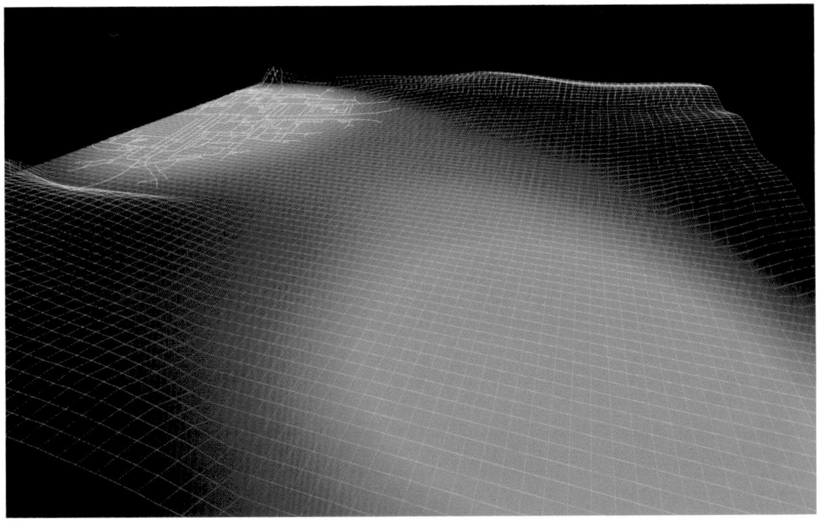

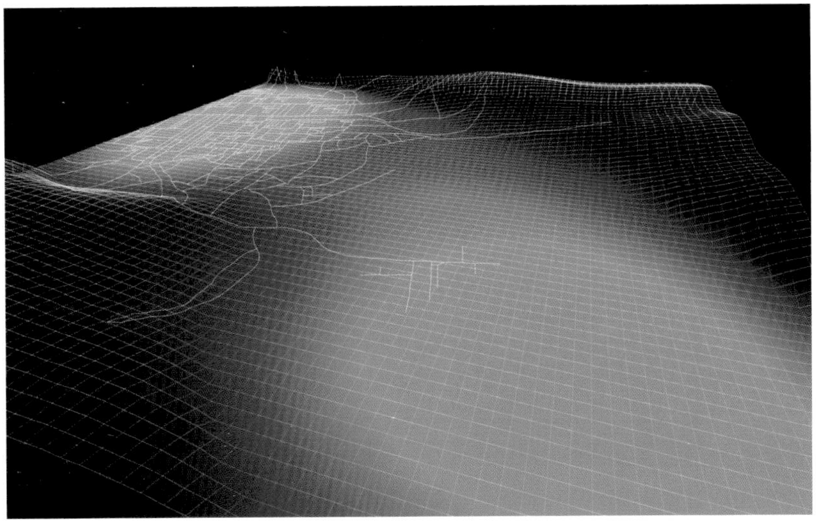

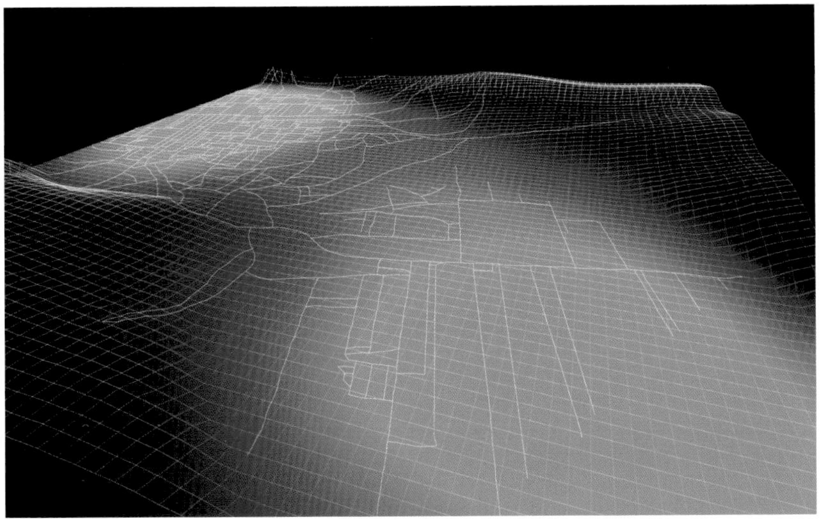

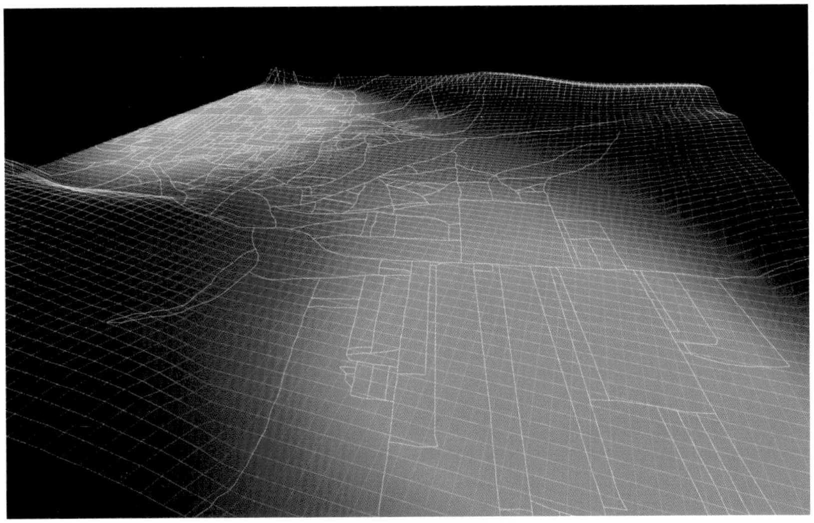

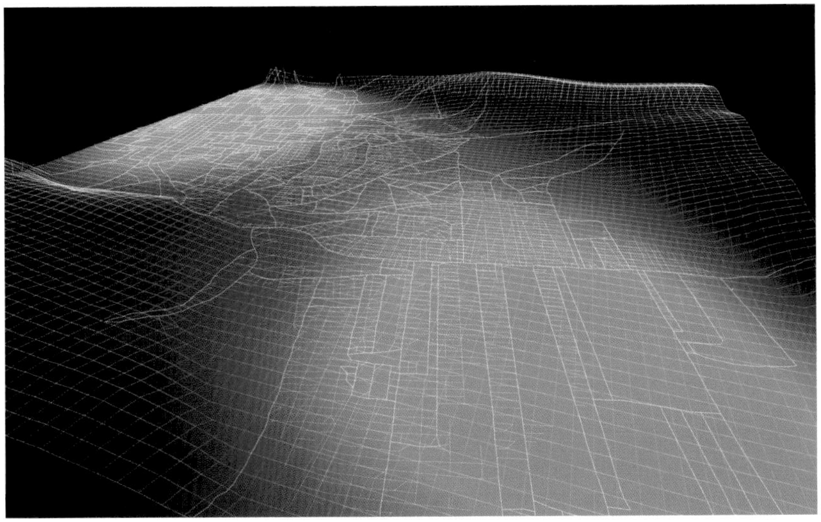

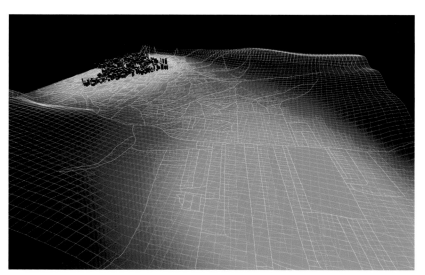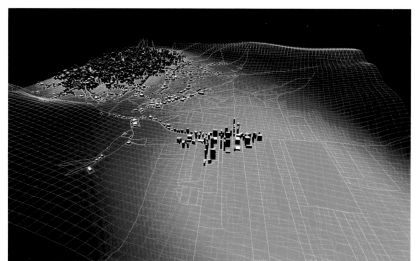

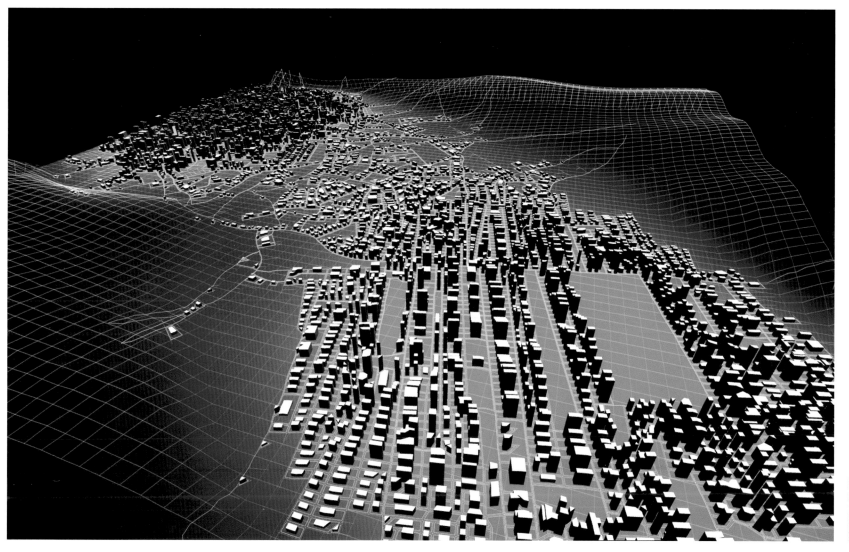

clockwise from top left
1, 2 & 3 Media Molecule studio interior.
4 The famous red door.
5 A presentation of how the levels will be sequenced and the art influences on them – prepared for a publisher visit.

MEDIA MOLECULE

www.mediamolecule.com

LOCATION
Guildford, UK

STAFF
18

KEY TITLE
Little Big Planet (2008)

ALONGSIDE THE FAMILIAR TALES OF NEXT-GEN DEVELOPMENT woes and the spiralling development costs that come with them, there's a ray of hope that is often identified as the most probable site of real innovation in videogames. Digital distribution has been touted for many years as the solution to a lot of the problems faced by modern developers. Boxless software, sold direct to the player – this surely has to play a key role in the future of the videogame industry. Sometime during the hyperbole about the arrival of this revolution, it happened. Xbox Live became a credible and rich platform for console distribution; mobile gaming identified itself as an obvious (if as yet not fully understood) cash-cow; and one of the most acclaimed developers of recent years, Valve (see pages 136–41), became a publisher with its Steam platform. For all the successes of the last few years, there are very few titles that demonstrate the promise of alternative videogame culture, digital distribution and simple word-of-mouth like *Rag Doll Kung Fu*.

Rag Doll Kung Fu feels like a working model of everything an 'alternative' game should be. It's built around a core, high-concept gameplay idea, which wouldn't be entertained by a mainstream publisher. Its art style is esoteric but beautiful, paying careful reference to the world it draws on with a lovingly produced in-game Super-8 kung fu movie. It even features explicit drug use as a gameplay mechanic. But it's important not to overlook that the whole enterprise is rendered with a care and precision that is rarely seen. It's not an exaggeration to say that you can palpably feel the love that went into the title when playing it. The small team that created *Rag Doll* obviously cares deeply about the experience the player has, and has made no compromise in making sure that it delivers its singular vision. It is intoxicating to be swept up in the joy the team felt in making it whilst playing it. Perhaps more than any release in the last few years, *Rag Doll Kung Fu* really exposes the humanity in game design. The creators are there in the game, dressed up in kung fu gear, fighting each other in Guildford Park, especially for you. You get the rare feeling that you're playing something as it was intended to be.

The release of *Rag Doll* on Steam was an important moment for online distribution. This new channel, instigated by one of the most important developer/publishers in the world today, was as lucky to get *Rag Doll* as *Rag Doll* was to get it. It ensured that Steam would be more than just a platform for *Half-Life* sequels (although that would have been fine) and PC port of console titles, making an important cultural statement about the future of videogames. It set a precedent, as Steam went on to feature more aggressively iconoclastic titles such as *Darwinia* and *The Ship*.

With the incorporation of a company and the commissioning of a major project for PlayStation 3, one might have suspected that the extraordinary creative character displayed in the team would be diluted beyond all recognition. But from the moment you enter Media Molecule's HQ, any fears you might have about a slide toward a corporate culture are immediately allayed. It's an expanding hive of activity. In the empty room next door to the studio, a trail of concept artwork snakes its way some 30 feet around the floor – up and down walls, over and under furniture. To follow the trail is to take a journey through the different aesthetic zones of the new project. 'We had a milestone meeting with the publisher and wanted to clearly explain the journey', explains Mark Healey – *Rag Doll Kung Fu* auteur and creative director at Media Molecule. The feeling is like being back at art school, except it is more fun and you don't have to write essays.

I spoke with Mark Healey (Creative and Technical Art Director); Alex Evans (Technical Director); Kareem Ettouney (Art Director) and Cathy Campos (PR). The interview takes place in the company's demo room, just as soon as the tea has been made. All three Media Molecule leads participate enthusiastically despite nursing hangovers from the previous night's Christmas party. As we start, Mark and Alex lead, and Kareem is intently drawing in his notebook.

*

Mark Healey Whenever we talk about anything around the studio, Kareem is always there sketching away.

Kareem Ettouney It really helps. This industry is full of very intelligent, imaginative people, and unless you capture

89

90

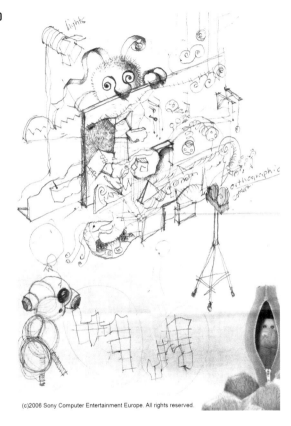

these ideas down really fast you end up having a really clever conversation, but that's all you have.

Can we back up slightly to the completion and release of *Rag Doll Kung Fu*? How did you get to be sat here as Media Molecule?

MH *Rag Doll Kung Fu* was made in our spare time – literally, evenings and weekends.

Alex Evans The project took about three years in total, but most of that was very laid-back. It was the final year after the GDC [Game Developer Conference] presentation in 2005 when things really took off.

MH That's when Kareem started at [acclaimed UK developer] Lionhead. It was his first weekend there and I asked him if he wanted to be in the kung fu film we were making.

KE I said of course! For them, of course!

Cathy Campos Although he did get very drunk and needed to be carried off the set.

AE The gin he's drinking in the movie is real gin.

KE It adds to the magic of the performance.

MH So we spent a weekend mucking around in the park in silly costumes, which sealed our relationship. This is the footage that appears in the game. I had the basis of *Rag Doll* in place, which I'd written while teaching myself C++, and Alex gave me some physics code to simulate ropes. I showed it to a few people at work after I made a prototype.

AE I still have the code. It's just a black screen with a triangle and a rope on it.

MH So we made a trailer for it. Somehow it got onto the Internet and caused a bit of a hoo-hah. But it was still very much a side project at this stage, and Peter [Molyneux – head of Lionhead Studios] was really cool about it, which we're really grateful for. That publicity really gave the project some momentum. Because of that, the people at GDC got wind and we were invited to show it at the experimental gaming workshop. We went there thinking it was just going to be a little thing, and there was a room with 500 people there. I winged the whole presentation, and it went down really well. Some people from Valve were in the audience and said they were interested in putting the game out on Steam, which was just gathering pace at that time. They flew me out to Seattle the next day and I met up with Gabe Newell. This was just when they decided they were going to start selling third-party games.

AE It was really useful for Valve, and good timing for everyone. Valve wanted to test more of what Steam was capable of, and we could try the whole thing out with a really fun, innovative and original title. This all meant that they could put it out with very low risk. It was a project that was nearly finished; I was a coder that they knew – it was a really good fit. They had the software development kit for Steam that they were just trying out and working out the documentation, and we became the first third-party game to be put out over the Steam network.

MH They became keen for us to go and work at Valve; they offered us jobs and flew us over to romance us.

AE I think it's worth mentioning, though, that we did talk to Lionhead early on about it being their project, but they didn't take it on. It wasn't that they didn't want it because they didn't like it. If you put it in the context of the time, they were so stretched; they were working on *Fable*, *Movies* and *Black and White 2*. The time just wasn't right.

MH Then we were in a situation where we have a contract with Valve to finish the game.

You're still at Lionhead now, right? You have full-time day jobs?

MH We were doing *Rag Doll* in the evenings and weekends after our day jobs. This was when Dave joined us on coding.

AE Within Lionhead we were working on a project that was announced at the same GDC where *Rag Doll* was. We came back to this scenario where Lionhead were crunching on *Black and White 2* and *Fable*, and we were getting on with *Rag Doll* at the same time. It was the worst possible combination of things, but it really cemented the relationship between all of us, which grew into Media Molecule. Two programmers and two artists – that dynamic and that communication really worked. It was a bit like living in a tent with your girlfriend. If you can survive that, you can survive anything, even moving in together. I worked on a lot of big projects, but you don't get the same team dynamic that you do on small things like this.

When most people describe crunch periods, they tend to be long, dark nights of the soul. This doesn't sound like that.

AE Because it was literally four of us, it just had to work.

KE Every one of us working on it had an angle that we were sharing because we were so close. Quite often in big projects these differing skills are all tucked away in different groups and they don't get cross-disciplinary input from each other. I think that's where the great work happens – from the collaboration.

AE I think there are a few studios trying to do that. There's one studio working on a large next-gen title that organizes its teams up into very small groups, and each one is very cross-discipline. So you'd have a concept artist and an animator and a programmer (or whatever is appropriate for that group) – it preserves that intimacy.

KE Any concept when it's first thought up just can't cover all of the possibilities, so that back and forth, that swapping of ideas, is a really important part of the process. The different skills need to be able to inspire and spark off each other. Mark has an art idea, I might see some way in which I can add to that, it goes back to Mark, Alex sees it's going to have an impact on the frame rate and makes a suggestion, somebody makes that work, the level designer sees that and thinks he can use this new art to make a new bit of fun. You need that fast swapping of ideas.

Do you think that's really contingent on having not just a small team, but a team with a really good, close relationship?

AE It's certainly hard to do on a large team. I think that's why you get so many breakaway studios. I think there's another

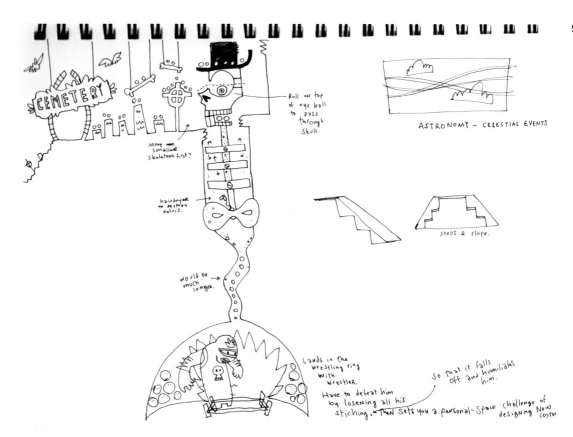

point to make here, which is that it really is a lot of work. People might have seen our presentations and Mark might come across as quite chaotic, but he's actually the most methodical artist I've ever worked with. He gave himself a task week of renaming all of the art files. It's almost obsessive-compulsive.

MH That just comes from the experience of working with lots of assets though – knowing how to save time later on.

KE It's almost a cliché to project that kind of crazy, chaotic image, and it always looks really cool – but that's not what gets games made. The real genius is a very fine balance between keeping rules and breaking rules, otherwise you

end up reinventing the wheel every day. It's important to make your history work for you. We try to use a lot of known techniques and build on them. Ironically, having those structures allows us to be more free in the areas where we want to be more experimental.

MH When we finished *Rag Doll*, Lionhead was coming to the end of a natural stage after *Fable*, and we talked about the opportunities to build on what we'd done. Alex was really excited about branching out, and it was me who was very tempted to stay at Lionhead. I had a job, I got paid well, I knew what I was doing. So the choice was, do I stay in this great job and get paid well doing something I love, or do I start something up with this lot and get loads of stress?

KE Clearly, you should do the second option.

MH We talked through lots of ideas together, and finally Alex managed to convince me.

AE It was very rapid. It was bizarre. We left Lionhead just before the Christmas party in December 2005. Then we were able to get a meeting with a publisher, Sony, which we hadn't really courted.

MH We had the opportunity to meet Phil Harrison [head of development for Sony Worldwide Studios] – fantastic.

AE We thought this was a one-off opportunity we couldn't pass up. We had a few ideas, so we put together a pretty vague pitch, if we're honest. We pitched it in December 2005, and we had our funding in place by the end of January 2006. We incorporated in February. It was just insanely fast. We spent January painting the offices. Everything happened literally in the space of a month. Suddenly you're buying desks and PCs and starting a studio. People ask us whether we went to lots of different publishers, and the honest answer is 'no'. We went to Sony, showed them this vague thing, and they just said 'Awesome. Go.' And even better than that, all the things we really wanted to do that we thought we'd tone down a little for the pitch because we thought they might be a little too weird, these were things he really picked up on, asking why we didn't do more of it. Traditionally, you don't pitch the weird stuff; you pitch the core idea as simply as you can – so it was great that he picked up on that.

KE I think one of the most crucial points to stress here is the chemistry of this team, the dynamics of the business. This studio couldn't exist without this huge investment in the relationship between the people in it. This is one of the big problems with the industry today – you can only get that through time.

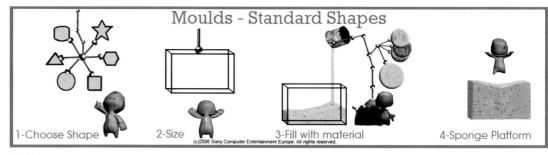

MH It's analogous to a band really.

AE It can come quickly though – our producer came over from Criterion, where she was working on *Burnout*, so she was used to working on a game a year, great games. We asked her to come over and help us on the structure side and she came along and instantly worked really well with all of us. We were used to working on these huge five-year projects where you basically kick back for the first three years and let it all sink in and experiment – which is great if you have the time – and she was used to this structured sequel process, so we are really getting the best of both worlds.

MH There's definitely still some chaos. We've managed to preserve that.

KE This is a great way of working, though. At Lionhead I was part of a central department that contributed to a lot of titles. You find that everything is separate for four years, and then in the last few months you start sticking things together. What we're trying to do isn't the opposite of that – you can't think of everything up front; games are too complicated for that. There are things that you can learn only through the process of doing them. For example, in areas of designing a character, there are known schools of thought on how to do that. But when it comes to designing an experience, you have to try things out and experiment. Where we can use knowledge that exists, we do.

In terms of that pitch, and in view of what you've just expressed about games being such a complex hybrid set of skills, how do you begin to describe what it is that you want to make?

MH We had a playable prototype that captured the essence of what we were trying to do.

AE The interesting thing is that there almost was no 'before'. It wasn't playable in a polished way. Basically, Kareem would sit down and sketch while there was a conversation going on, and capture ideas.

Before you had the prototype, how did you know what you were going to make?

MH I remember the first moment when we talked about this game, actually. We went to the cinema to see *Howl's Moving Castle*, and I was chatting with Dave and saying how it would be cool to have character controls – a bit like *Rag Doll*, but on a console – and we had a notion of how it would control.

AE It was a combination of some very quick conversations, a few sketches and a quick playable demo where you could hold a PS2 pad, plug it into a PC and try it out. I wrote a program with Dave that allowed you to run through concept art, so you got the feeling of being in control of the game, you could feel the kind of inertia and sense the kind of art style.

KE The great thing about this industry is that it makes people become more hybrid. Alex isn't just a coder; he's a great artist. Mark isn't just an artist; he's a coder – that kind of hybrid practitioner working on something really helps to create a great hybrid product.

AE One of the other things about the pitch process was that we were pitching ourselves partly, because we didn't have much to show at such short notice. Mark's been in the industry for 15 years, I've been in it for ten, Kareem has enormous experience and brings in all these other skills. So the first half of the pitch was the story of *Rag Doll*, where we built up to showing the demo. An important thing to note is that we always use our own tools to show our work – we never use PowerPoint. So you can literally have concept art side by side with data side by side with the actual character running around.

MH I think that was one of the big things that impressed them; that we showed something actual we could make while pitching.

AE One of the things Sony really liked about *Rag Doll* is that users were able to express themselves so easily. That was something they really wanted to preserve and develop. The other big question was, 'how do we translate the mouse-driven physics of something like *Rag Doll* onto a controller?' Conveniently, that was one of the things we were able to answer first, from Dave's prototype. If someone just asked that question and we showed them a piece of paper explaining it, it wouldn't really make sense. They asked the question, and seconds later we were able to hand them the controller to pass around and they were able to feel it. Obviously, it's a million miles away from anything you'd ever ship, but it allowed them to understand what we were aiming for. Then when they asked what the visual style of the game is, the character was able to walk through the concept painting that Kareem had just done for us. Then, when the discussion was about feature-sets, in our case it's about online features, and although we couldn't plug the demo into the Internet, we could visually show what we were planning.

That's something we've always tried to do since – make a demo to that level – which I haven't seen many other people do. We tend to commit early to prototypes rather than go into documents. The prototype is actually about proving the really simple and most important questions. Then we start trying to structure it.

MH The interesting point for me is that how you present something is hugely important. We could have gone in with a Word document or something, but people don't want to have to imagine that much. Making something that's really slick and fun is really important. It's not enough to just have a great idea in your head and tell people 'trust me! It's going to be cool!'

AE With *Rag Doll*, when you're just four people it's very easy to communicate. Even when you scale to 20, you can be saying something and it can be the most obvious thing, but to someone else it can be cloudy and complicated, so we tend to go for visual prototypes as quickly as possible.

KE It really helps whenever we have any conversation. Last week we were having a discussion about a feature and whether we should have it or not. You really want to be able to see application of that feature and understand what you're going to lose and gain right then, at that instant. It's so important to be able to communicate these things in the right way. Mark sometimes will show new ideas with a bit of video, or Alex will have a small bit of code that does something to communicate an idea.

AE It backfired on us once though. Sometimes, especially to an audience that isn't fully part of the team, if you present something that's quite slick they can assume that it's the final thing. We had an early video that was simultaneously one of the best things we did and one of the biggest albatrosses. It was this 2D-into-3D thing. Our game is beautifully 3D-rendered, but a lot of our concept had been 2D and the physics of the game are mainly 2D. Mark made a bit of video

to show how this was going to work. But of course, because it was sufficiently highly rendered and looked really nice, it became the only thing that people could latch on to and think, 'right, that's what the game's going to look like.' I remember halfway through the prototyping phase we'd already massively exceeded it, and people were still thinking that was what it was going to look like.

KE It's a stepping stone image, though. People like slogans, icons, things to latch on to. If people were to ask me what something looks like, I find it very different to summarize. People latched on to that presentation and thought it was iconic of the project, but that's what people need.

AE There's a price to making these slick visuals early on. People latch.

KE I like the risk of it, personally. It forces you to improve. If you show someone something and they like it, if you want to move away from it then you have to do something better. It's subjective, but it forces you to make decisions and not postpone. You build on what you have and slowly build a vocabulary; you show people an evolution. An architect shows a sketch, then a watercolour, then a 3D fly-through etc. As long as there is evolution it's not harmful.

MH I'm trying to improve communicating ideas clearly. For example, we're talking about a menu system. The fact that it's a visual thing means you *have* to do a visual take on it. But you have to really clearly show people that 'THIS IS SHOWING THE MENU TREE IT IS NOT A VISUAL TREATMENT OF IT'. Otherwise you get people looking at it and not looking at the content.

KE 'Why is it blue!?'

AE Our initial pitch to Sony was all hand-drawn. As Kareem says, sometimes the risk pays off – the video was ultimately a risk worth taking.

MH It's easy to be scared to actually make a mark, to actually do something. It's easy to talk about things in a blue-sky kind of way, I think it's really important to actually do things.

AE There was a lesson we learnt at Lionhead actually. Dave and I worked really well together and evolved a really close language. We had this thing he did called 'hacking', where we'd sketch out an idea of code together, but it turned out that when we said 'hacking' to other people, they misunderstood it to mean 'messy code'. So we'd say to them, 'can you implement this feature and just hack it in?', which to Dave and I meant, 'can you spend a lot of time and care on this and then do the minimum possible to prove the idea with elegant code.' We didn't mean, 'just lash it together'.

KE It's a serious issue. I've seen a lot of huge arguments just because of interpretation.

AE Sure. You get as much of that visually as you do with spoken language.

The absence of motion, of feedback is a crippling problem. It's a real frustration with screenshots – they're so profoundly undescriptive of the game.

AE Sure. In film, the frame leads the eye obviously. However, in game cameras, sometimes we are really zoomed out for gameplay reasons. But when you look at a static screenshot where you're not playing, there's no context because you don't have any idea of where you should be focused. What you see on screen is really complex, emerging visual feedback that is being given specifically to that player in that moment based on what they're actually doing – that cannot possibly translate.

How would you characterize your work as Media Molecule?

MH I'd like to think we're slick, original and innovative. I think we have a big appetite for doing things that are slightly more 'out there', but we're doing it very well, with really high production values.

AE I think it's the belief that there are loads of ideas out there that haven't been exploited yet. It's not like we're inventing the things that we're doing – we just choose to do them in a fresh way. Whenever we try to describe our work in terms of other games it always fucks up. If you describe *Rag Doll* as a beat-em-up, that doesn't really capture what it is. You asked about when we go into a pitch – how do we describe the work. That elevator pitch thing is one of the things we're worst at, which is probably also one of our great assets.

Do you think there's something quite English about your work? I mean that in a positive way.

AE A kind of esoteria?

There's an obvious commitment to the detail of its own world, its own internal weird logic. There's this real intoxication and joyous abandon about it – kind of like the feeling from *LEGO Star Wars*. There's a real Media Molecule signature emerging; you can see your fingerprints on your work.

AE I'm happy with the joyous tag. One of the biggest things we got from playtesting is it's really funny because people laugh.

MH I'm a big fan of people laughing with games.

AE A big thing that's informing our view of online play is that it shouldn't be just person versus person – it should be sofa versus sofa. You might get four mates who choose to play together going online and seeing what's going on; you get these little local and distributed social clubs emerging. You get the joy in the room, but also get to share it.

MH I think giving people the tools to play creatively together is so important.

AE A big thing with *Rag Doll* was people being able to skin their own characters. You'd think that most people would just use the flickbook feature to make characters, but the stats were showing that loads of people were really putting in the time to make their own.

MH You can get the shit kicked out of you by David Hasselhoff. People are *incredibly* creative.

this page Two instructive posters explain some of the key concepts of *Little Big Planet*.

95

Better With a Friend

Support your friends
Characters act as physical bodies in the world, so you can stand on each others shoulders.
It also means your friends can sometimes get in the way!

Hangers on
Grab onto to each others legs, and form amazing gymnastic feats. Very handy for getting to those difficult to reach places.

Carrying your friends
Like other objects in the world, characters can also be carried. And thrown.....

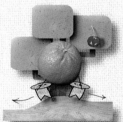

Rolling Along...
With team effort,, pulling objects can help you make somel novel forms of transport.

Many Hands...
Heavy objects are easier to pick up when you anothe rpair of hands.

Breaking up...
In some situations, you really need a friend. Som eobjects in the world can literally Be pulled apart.

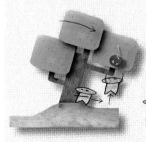

Pushing/Pulling
By pulling some bendy objects, yo ucan make attractive items easier to reach.

Lift me up
Some devices in the world require more than one character to operate.
Various pulleys, cogs, and switches can make some mad contraptions.

Playing with toys
Sometimes having a freind can make certain objects more fun. There are various toys to find in the storys, from a football, to musical instruments - all can be interacted with in a simple way.

Basic Tools to Collect

Chainsaw
Cuts polystyrene ,wood.

Spray Paint
Can spray on cloth materials

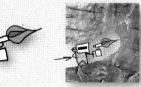

Chainsaw - Rip through wood and polystyrene with this awesome collection of teeth and speed!
Be careful when cutting shapes though, as isolated shapes will fall!

Spray Paint - From tagging your name, to making a fine mural, this baby coms in a selection of colours. Simply clamber over the cloth, and spray at will!

Scissors
Cuts cloth materials

Blow Torch
Cuts metal

Scissors - Just the thing you need for cutting out luvly shapes, which can be used to decorate the world around you, and yourself!
Large shapes will require you to clamber over the cloth, smaller shapes will zoom camera in, so you can be more refined!

Blow Torch - A chainsaw isn't going to d othe job here - you need oure heat. Same interface as chainsaw, but watch out for hot metal! Cutting through metal safely can be a lengthy process!

Diamond Glass Cutter
Cuts Glass

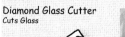

Glue
For sticking decorations, maybe objects to objects?

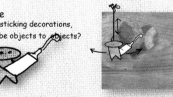

Diamond Glass Cutter - Cutting glass can be a tricky process, slipping and sliding all over the place, this tool makes life easier for you.

Glue, so, you've have lots of nice decorations looking for a home, well, you can use glue, to stick your bits and bobs in all kinds of places.

MEDIA MOLECULE

this spread Level concepts reveal a huge amount of detail about the playable design, art style and wit of the game.

level design _ Template
Important Note: To Guide the players through the puzzles We use Cut scenes, information tips, stickers with information…etc
Important Note: The dimensions of the platforms in this Layout are rough and not schematic, they can be longer or shorter According to how it feels to play..
Colectable
More Cactus game play
Remove the small rocks Then push the massive one to kill the ant eater !!! which allows the ants to pass safely In the dense cactus area below (with you riding on them)
You can go straight to the other side from here if you have 8 players, cooperating together to push this massive bridge
Push ledge to block the falling rocks
Secret cave full of collectable rescores
Lower the lift to help your friends up or they'll have to wait for the ant that takes longer
Bats chase & push you
Very cool colectable Takes a lot of skill to get up there...
Wheeyyy :) now you got your wagon to this point, the lift is activated to take you up without the wagon it dosnt work..
Ant eater which eats the ants that are the only way to pass on the thick cactus!!!
Use gecko toungs as platforms
Jump up and down to operate the push wagon (much easier with two people)
Place marshmallows on spikes to make safe Path
Pull the switch to lower the bridge ..
Start
ah ha you can pass here but your wagon is left behind until you sort out those falling rocks by going up there.
Make your way through the dangerous cactus
* Avoid cactus spikes
*Find safe bald patches
*Collect material balls
*Collect Cactus paper flowers to decorate your piñata in your Personal space.
Very Dense Cactus that you can not get through without riding on the ants.... ....But the evil Ant Eater keeps eating them and stopping you from progressing!!
Grab onto the ant that climbs the wall, but only one player can go at a time
Bats chase & push you
Falling rocks that obstruct your path and can destroy your wagon ,every time you push one away another one falls from the aztec masks mouth....!
This Secret cave is hidden Until you pass this point.
Secret cave full of collectable rescores
Back
If you fall here you die (comedy death) and respawn in the last check point, if you are skilled you can Land on the rock in the middle and jump back to safety.
(c)2006 Sony Computer Entertainment Europe. All rights reserved.

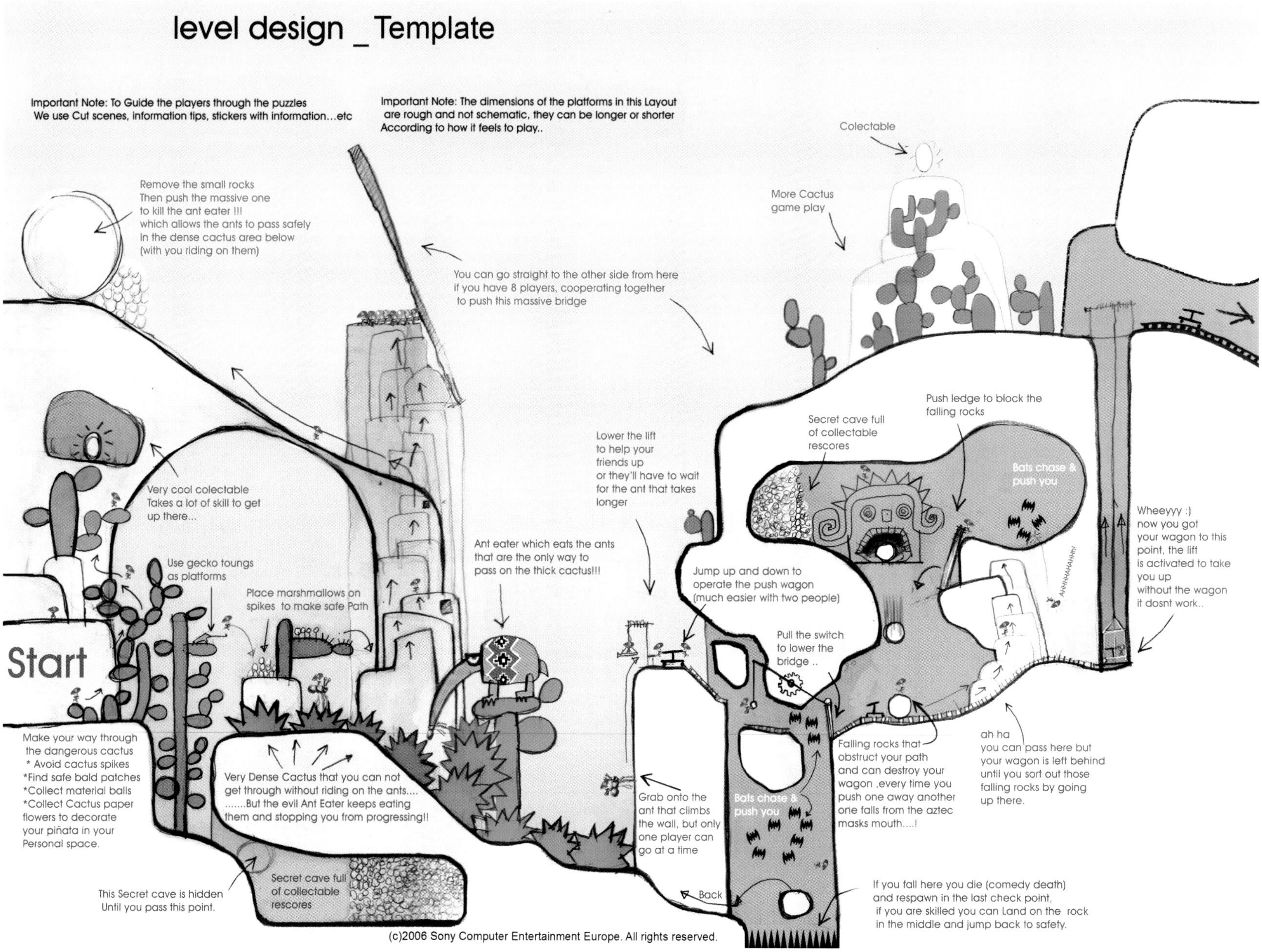

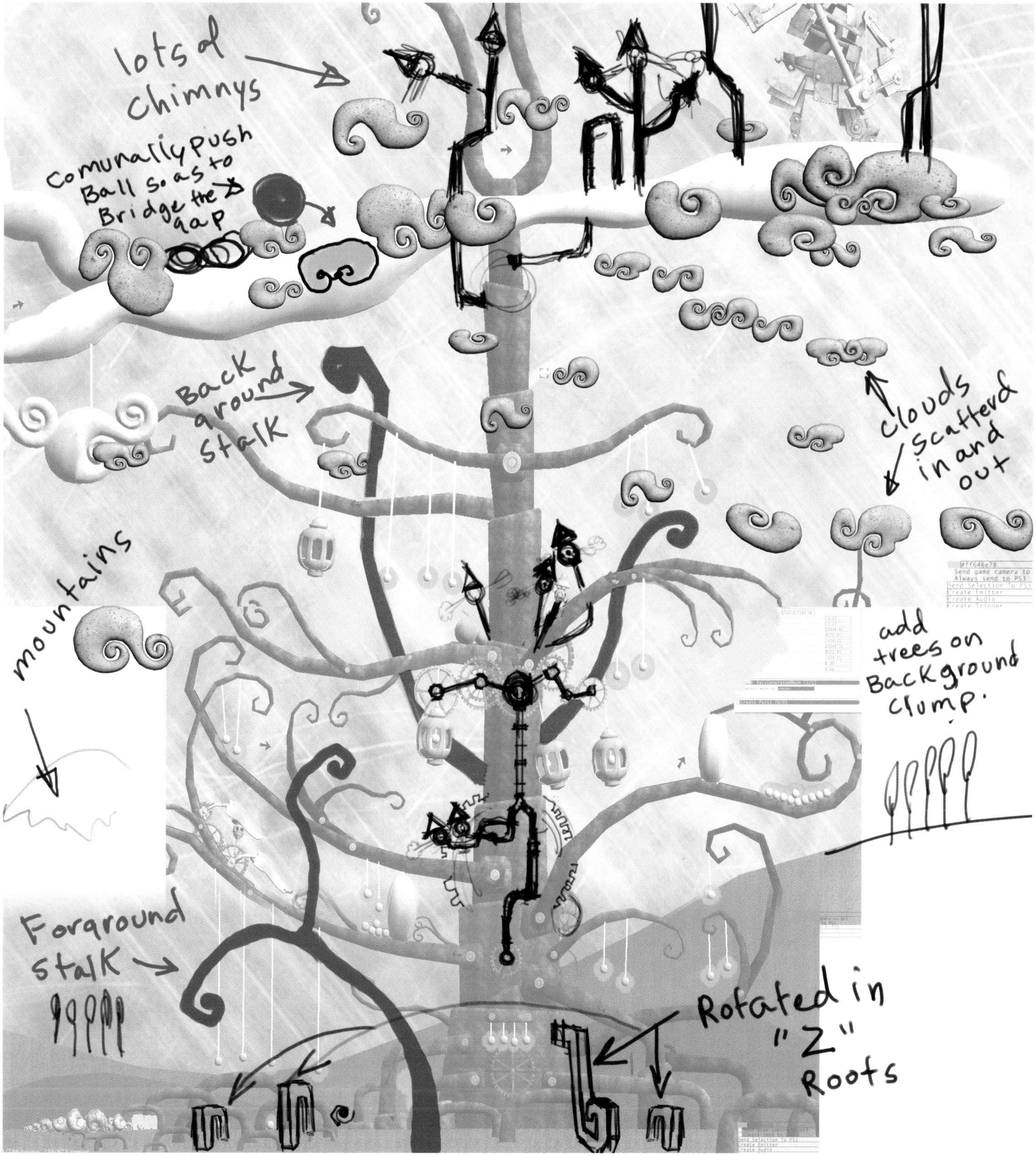

lots of chimnys

comunally push Balls.as to Bridge the gap

Back ground stalk

mountains

clouds scatterd in and out

add trees on Background clump.

Foreground stalk

Rotated in "Z" Roofs

this page 'SackBoy' and his friends test out the real-world physics in these screenshots from the Game Developer Conference 2007 demo of *Little Big Planet*.

this page The high-def rendering of lo-fi real-world materials gives *Little Big Planet* a unique aesthetic — kitchen-table hobbycraft colliding with cutting-edge game development.

99

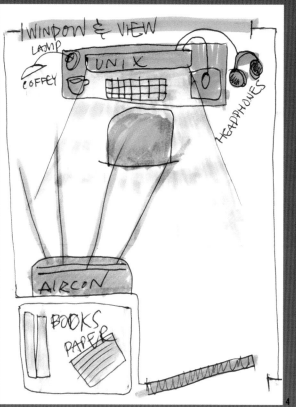

clockwise from top left
1 Hampus Söderström's workstation.
2 Söderström
3 A *Toribash* promotional poster.
4 Söderström's studio plan.

NABI STUDIOS

www.toribash.com

LOCATION
Singapore

STAFF
3

KEY TITLE
Toribash (2006)

'STRATEGIC TURN-BASED FIGHTING... THE GAME FEATURES physics, full dismemberment, decapitation and comic-style blood.' *Toribash*, like *Rag Doll Kung Fu* (with which it shares a number of characteristics), has a particularly pure concept. Like *Rag Doll Kung Fu* (see pages 89–94), this also feels like a game that is particularly representative of the best of what independent games could be. Its creator, Hampus Söderström, made his videogame debut with this extraordinary title.

Toribash takes the beat-em-up genre, a staple of the arcade tradition often characterized by frantic 'button-mashing', and slows it down to a considered exchange of turns. Making no concessions to those who might want to 'pick-up-and-play', *Toribash* forces a forensic attention to detail on the body of your fighter. Limbs are twisted, aimed and loaded with energy before being fired as an attack at your opponent. It's at that moment that the game rewards you with a viscerally compelling display of bone-crunching violence and splatter-flick gore. And make no mistake, it *is* a display. Like *Porrasturvat* (*Stair Dismount*) before it, once the scene has been set and the variables for limb movement declared the player is invited to sit back and enjoy the ballet of violence they have choreographed. It's difficult not to squirm with guilty pleasure as the fighting plays out. The *Toribash* community has become a rich seam of highly imaginative user-created carnage as players use the game to capture ever more elaborate attacks to movie files for sharing with each other.

As the awards rain down on the project, Söderström is concentrating on the next iteration of the *Toribash* project. He corresponded with me by email shortly before flying out to the Slamdance game festival.

Could you tell me a little about how you came to make *Toribash*?

I have a background as an IT consultant, mostly working with Unix-related consulting. My other projects include music software, P2P and database-software development (www.hampusdb.org). *Toribash* is my first game project and the first project of my new studio, Nabi Studios Pte Ltd.

Being trained as a Unix programmer has certainly had influences on my ruthless, and at times unpopular, approach to simplicity.

Why code? What attracts you to it?

I like to code because it is very direct and it combines engineering, creativity and design. Coding also has the great advantage of being 'provable'. In programming, a good idea is close to worthless without the actual codes proving the idea. Code talks, bullshit walks! It is the same with simulations. You don't know how something really works until you have successfully implemented it. This is what I like about programming. I often have arguments with fellow programmers about how to implement something. You often hear, 'That's easy. You just do this and that.' But at the end of the day, when you sit there with the actual implementation, a whole world of different problems appears.

How did the core concept for *Toribash* emerge?

Toribash was an idea formed by combining several other existing concepts into a new one. For me, it seems to be a passive process – something that happens unconsciously while I am doing something else. I've also noticed that I have the best ideas for a certain project when I am busy on another project. I don't believe in being too novel. Ten per cent new idea should be enough for something to feel fresh and new.

How did you begin to capture your initial ideas? Were these visual sketches or written design docs?

I like to do drawings of an idea in a sketchbook and I also talk about the idea over IM with friends. After that, I do the initial research on code libraries, technologies and similar software. It does not take long before I start writing the first line of codes.

Can you precis the development process of the game, in terms of broad stages and people involved?

I have a core group of testers and the graphic artist Nokturnal that I work with. I send them the programs for testing in an early stage. I always like to release early to get some sort of feedback loop going as soon as possible. When the program is starting to get ready, I contact a designer to do any graphics elements and add a website to the program.

Toribash **is so pure in its conception, I imagine that sharing ideas with collaborators (were there any?) was fairly straightforward?**

The game concept was easily shared and understood by my collaborators (friends, game players, testers, graphic designer), even though the game didn't initially fit into any specific genre.

Can you talk me through the visual design of the game? The fierce minimalism serves it fantastically well; how did you arrive at that? Was it as deliberate as it feels, or would you rather have set the game within a lush 3D stage environment?

I followed the motto that any feature that doesn't add to the game simply makes it worse. It enabled us to focus 90 per cent on gameplay and to finish the game in a reasonable amount of time.

The simplicity is both deliberate and a necessity. I do not have the resources to make a game that looks like the latest Japanese console fighting game. This restriction forces you to compete on other terms, preferably with the gameplay. I may not be able to add a glossy environment, but, I will make the game playable on a slow Internet connection.

Following on with the discussion of the visual, could you tell me about some of the influences on the game's visual design, from wherever they might come from?

The design document of *Toribash* mentions the English design group TokyoPlastic (who made the Drum Machine Flash Movie); Vinyl dolls; and the Matrix 'loader program' as inspiration for the visuals.

To come up with the simple control mechanism of the characters in *Toribash* took a lot of effort. I think I released ten versions before it finally worked. Unless I figured out how to control the characters, all the backgrounds in the world would not make the game playable.

Even if you scope the game painfully simple, you will soon realize that your schedule is fully packed with other aspects of maintaining and commercializing a game: maintaining servers, writing payment interfaces, creating online ranking scripts, making customizations for portals, writing press releases, handling support and so on.

What were the elements of fighting that you most wanted to capture in the game and how successful do you think you were?

I wanted to combine the strategic part of fighting with the possibility of doing impossible moves. I never thought that the game would be 'unintentionally hilarious', as one of the first players described it. This is a very pleasant surprise and adds a great value to the game.

Like *Stair Dismount* **before it,** *Toribash* **succeeds spectacularly in making the player** *feel* **the extraordinary violence being meted out. Can you tell me why this is so effective? What makes** *Toribash* **hurt so much?**

I think it must be the dismemberment sound that makes it so painful. One of the collaborators, Deerslayer, was there when I added the sound and we both laughed when we saw the first replay using it. It just looked so painful yet made you so happy.

The game feels like it's exactly how you wanted it to be, with little or no compromise, which is one of the things that makes it so compelling. Is that the case?

The long-term plan was to make the first *Toribash* game fun, the sequel good-looking and the third realistic. There are no compromises in terms of the core gameplay. However, there are many technical compromises to achieve real-time simulation speed.

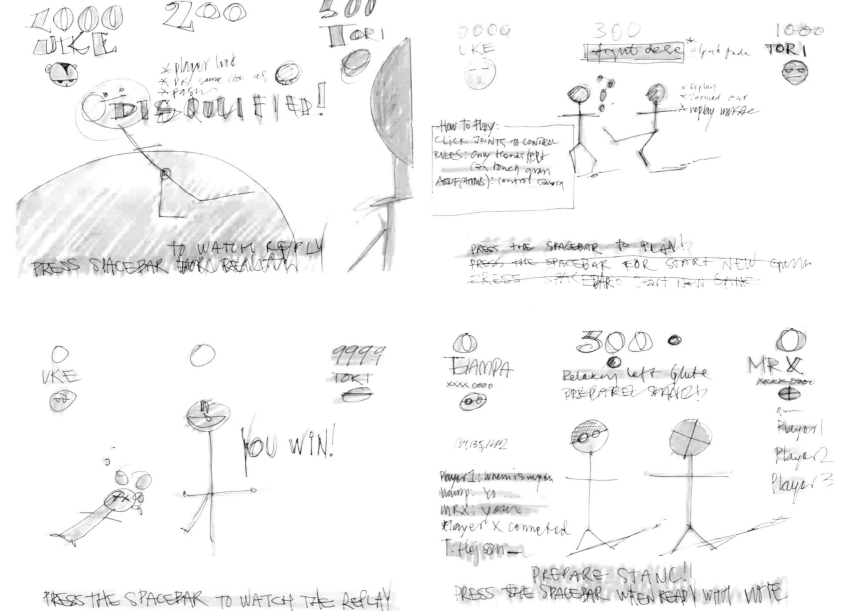

this spread *Toribash* is entertainingly effective in its ability to get the player to feel the crunch of the violence taking place. Its minimal design forces the player to focus on the physicality of what is happening.

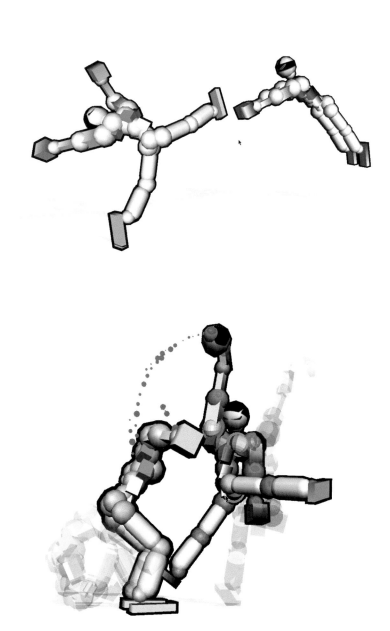

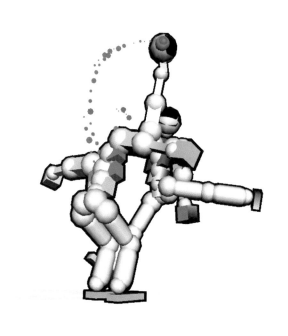

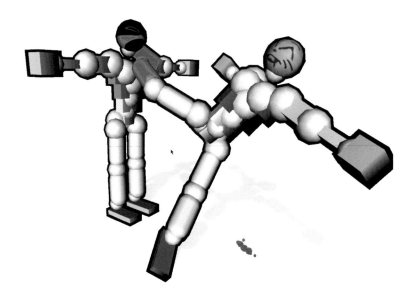

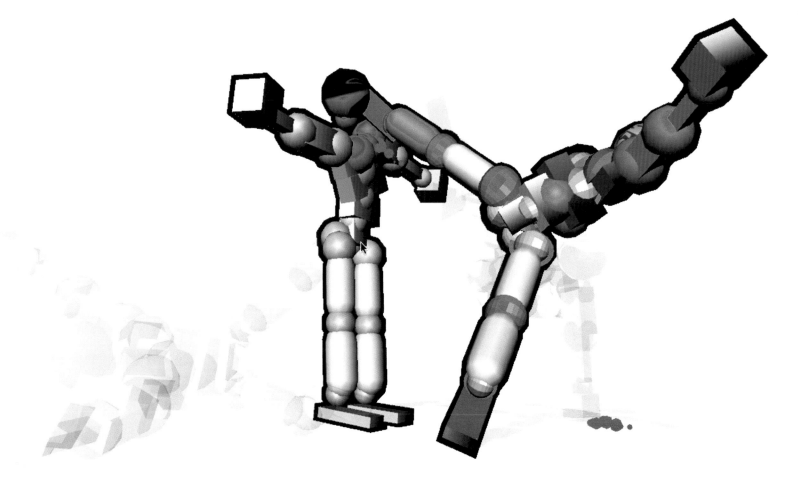

1

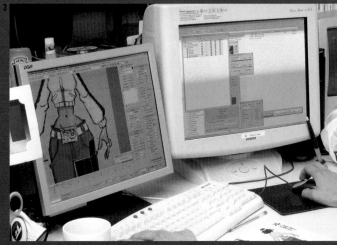

2

3

4

6

5

clockwise from top left
1 Relentless Studios.
2 David Amor (Creative Director) and
Andrew Eades (Development Director).
3 Relentless Studios.
4 *Buzz* artwork in context.
5 & 6 Relentless Studios.

RELENTLESS SOFTWARE

www.relentless.co.uk

LOCATION
Brighton, UK

STAFF
45

KEY TITLES
Buzz! The Big Quiz (2006)
Buzz! The Music Quiz (2005)
DJ Decks and FX (2004)

SELECTED AWARDS
BAFTA Winner, Best Casual and Social Game, *Buzz!*
The Big Quiz (2006)
BAFTA Nominee, Best Audio, *DJ Decks and FX* (2004)

'IT'S NOT A PARTICULAR *EFFORT* TO BE DIFFERENT TO EVERYONE else. It just happens that we are.'

Andrew Eades is the co-founder of Relentless Software. Along with David Amor, he formed the company as a direct response to several decades of hard lessons in the trenches of trying to make videogames. The company has a hardline attitude towards working practices and is producing BAFTA (British Academy of Film and Television Arts)-winning games in one of the most interesting and potentially lucrative areas of the games market.

Relentless was constituted extremely quickly, in a development deal that was an unusual example of circumstance and rapid corporate decision-making aligning to the greater good. Amor and Eades are deeply committed to their company and the products it produces.

Relentless is almost as well known in the industry for its vocal disapproval of the old-school game-development style of project management, which involved 'crunches' during which workers would simply work until the job was done, resulting in poor work, personal misery and high levels of stress. In conspicuously trying to do things differently, Amor and Eades have put their process where their money is. So far, this approach appears to be paying off.

Relentless is one of the leaders in the emerging 'social' games market. In recognition that millions of homes own PlayStations, but few members of the family other than the kids are actually playing on them, a new wave of software is being developed that will engage wider audiences in interactive entertainment. To date, this has been pioneered on PS2 by Sony Europe with titles such as *Singstar* and *EyeToy*. Nintendo are also doing huge amounts of work in this area. With the standard game controller being a very intimidating and complex device for non-gamers, these games, by the use of a different controller bundled in the box, broke down the barriers between the game and the player. *Singstar* was a karaoke game that supplied the players with a microphone; *EyeToy* was a game that came supplied with a camera, allowing players to control the games with their bodies. *Buzz*, Relentless's breakthrough title, was a quiz game that came bundled with four big red buzzers.

Instantly visible and understandable from across a shop floor, Relentless hit the mainstream in October 2005 when *Buzz* was launched. Five months later, it shipped the sequel, *Buzz!: The Big Quiz*. The company is currently working on more, as yet unannounced, *Buzz* titles.

Amor and Eades both spent several years in the games industry at some of the most important companies: EA, Virgin, DMA and Mindscape. They first met when Amor interviewed Eades for a lead programmer job on a title he was working on at the new Computer Artworks studio he had set up in Brighton. A *DJ* title commissioned by Sony Europe, it was stimulating enough for Eades to drop his salary expectations to come to work there. But Computer Artworks faced grave financial troubles: a few months into the project a midnight meeting was called and the managers, of whom Amor was one, were told to break the news to the staff that they wouldn't be being paid that month.

As the company collapsed, Amor and Eades hatched a plan to pitch completion of the *DJ* title to Sony. To their surprise, Sony accepted and a new studio was born within 36 hours.

I met with them at their Brighton studio where they were candid and relaxed. The first hours of Relentless Software are being remembered.

David Amor So hurriedly, in my spare bedroom, we had an afternoon to open a bank account so Sony could pay us, then we needed to come up with a name for the company. As we were full of determination that afternoon, we put 'unstoppable' into the thesaurus. The idea was that rather than 'aim for milestones, miss, have another go', our aim was 'slow and steady wins the race'. So we set up Relentless, as suggested by the thesaurus. We got the team together and told them, 'we know it's a risk, but Sony will pay us, we will be able to pay you this month, but if you stick around we think we can make this work out.' Rather than rush right back into it, we really thought about our process from scratch. The Internet, for example is a distraction – those messages popping up all the time just eats into time. We all felt that if we turned up to work and actually worked

107

108 rather than treating it like a youth club, people could probably go home on time.

We wanted a company that was going to meet its milestones. We wanted to wow the publishers so that they would place a second product with us. We had no idea if we'd still be around in a year's time – if you'd asked me then, I'd have said it was 50/50. But the best way of improving those odds was to do a good job. I said, 'I'm sick of working late; I'm sure you are too. Let's fix it.'

Andrew Eades After a dozen or so years in the industry, I've never seen crunches work, ever. And if they do, the week afterwards everyone's useless. But even then – everyone was shocked; 'you mean we have to get in at nine!?'

DA It's weird the way videogame culture has evolved. From [Steve] Wozniak and [Steve] Jobs working in the garage all night, it's evolved as if that's normal. In other jobs it's not like this. Digging roads, you dig from nine to five until the hole is dug, and then you go home.

AE There's an idea that to be creative you need to have access to the Internet. It's not true. Never has been true. Never will be true.

So how come the answer you still get from a lot of studios about crunches and working conditions is still, 'well, we think we need to have people willing to go the extra mile' – as a euphemism for working overtime?

DA Why don't you just work out how many miles you want to do, and plan for them?

That seems obvious to anyone who's ever worked on any project in any industry. So how come you appear to be one of the few companies who are practising this?

AE You have to be an absolute true believer. I think a lot of businesses are run by people who have worked all the hours

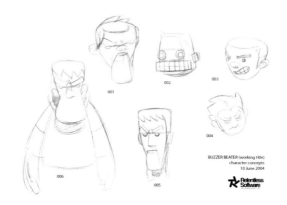

BUZZER BEATER (working title)
character concepts
10 June 2004
Relentless Software

God sends, but have no idea what it's like to be an employee. There are some people here who are shocked when they're sent home at five because they've never done that, after ten years in the industry. And we say, 'well, you're going to have to find a hobby or something.'

DA One of our programmers was saying, 'I don't really know what to do when I go home, though', and he was sad. But – and maybe this is because we're making social games – I don't want a lot of people on the edge working for us. The industry has suffered from making games for itself. Geeks making games for geeks, to be unkind.

AE If you don't plan properly, you will fail. And then you fail again and again – and then it becomes normal. Deadlines mean nothing to a lot of developers. But to us it's fundamental. We deliver milestones on time, in person and hopefully with a few little extras that we can squeeze in. In order to do that, you have to plan.

Are there are any positive models you have based your studio on, or is Relentless in fact a response to seeing how you didn't want things to be done?

DA We worked out what we wanted to do by seeing a number of things fail. By looking at the things that were broken, we looked at what we could fix. To be fair, there's

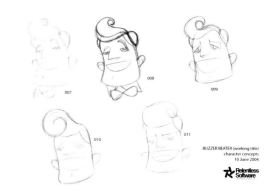

BUZZER BEATER (working title)
character concepts
10 June 2004
Relentless Software

loads of existing stuff from videogame culture that we took with us.

As you describe your philosophy, it sounds almost conservative, whereas within videogame production it's pretty radical.

DA There's some camaraderie that we miss out on from not playing Quake during the day, but that's why we put on a lot of events. Each year we go away abroad on holiday, with all partners invited. The money we spend doing those things is a fraction of what it would cost us to miss a milestone. We have a lot of extra-curricular things that happen deliberately. We always invite people's partners. My wife never really knew anybody else from my work, but a number of things happen when women turn up. If it's just the workers who turn up, the conversation is just about work all night. When it's a proper social occasion, my wife won't tolerate videogame conversation, which has got to be a good thing. That works well.

What are the most important things about Relentless for you?

AE This is the most rewarding job I've ever had, and I like having large amounts of control. It's a real vindication of everything I believe in. I've tried so many systems for project management, and the only one that works is the one here. I don't have the frustrations of answering hundreds of emails

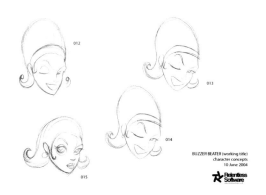

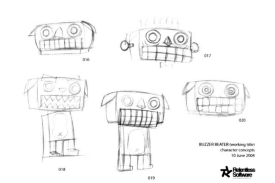

BUZZER BEATER (working title)
character concepts
10 June 2004

Relentless
Software

Is it important to you that you, as a developer, are quite visible to the consumer? That people recognize Relentless as well as *Buzz*? Your character as a studio is very visible.

AE We keep a high profile mainly so that when we recruit people, they've heard of us. But also I'd like to think that if Relentless is on the box, people know what they're getting.

But you're outspoken, compared to most studios.

AE We've got good PR.

Well, you're often expressing an actual opinion.

AE It's not a particular effort to be different from everyone else. It just happens that we are. If you've worked in the industry as long as we have, it's a rough old place, full of hard-luck stories – but why should it be? We can control our little bit. It's my industry as much as it is the most senior VP at EA's industry. I've been in it all my life and I've got as much of a right as anyone to say what I think about it.

But don't you get a little bored of the standard apologist stance of the games industry?

AE 'Sorry, we make games.'

Absolutely.

AE But we've been sneered at for so many years. I remember going to university and telling girls I was studying philosophy rather than computer science, because I thought I'd get more action. But now, of course, we're in the year of the geek.

How did *Buzz* come about?

DA A company called Sleepydog had approached Sony and said, 'we've got all these music clips, perhaps you'd like to

---

a day. I don't have the frustrations of not quite understanding why my managers are asking me to do something. Having been a high-performing employee who can't get their message through, and now also being a manager stressed about getting people paid, I think I've got a good understanding of how to do this now.

Making hit games is a very difficult thing to do deliberately, and you end up struggling to make mediocre games. I always felt I should be making better games than I was. I just couldn't figure out why I wasn't making the best games in the world. But you need the right structure in order to be able to do it.

In view of the way that you work and the culture you've established, what does growth mean to you? In terms of size, is that kind of growth a threat to the culture you've established?

AE I don't have an answer to that. When we started we had 12 people, and we thought we'd grow to a massive 18 people. David and I both had lots of different hats on, but then reality hit that there were projects available but we weren't big enough to support them. Publishers want to spend their money on what they think is a good opportunity.

We're aiming to expand a bit. We might go to 50, but we've grown really fast and I'd quite like a little period of chill-out when we're just steady. I'd like us to do a game a year at least, and we keep slotting titles into our release

---

schedule – I like the size we are now. It's very easy for David and me to get dragged so far into a project that we lose our strategic view. We need to release ourselves from the critical path completely. We had to prove it. You can make great games without killing staff and eating pizza all night. I'm proud to say we do have a no pizza policy.

So, what are the biggest threats?

AE Making sure that our culture doesn't just erode bit by bit. New people coming in weren't here at the painful birth, so they don't know what we've been through. The fact is that all of this is fine as long as we're successful. The moment we fail – well, I don't know what would happen. But I don't plan on it happening either.

How vulnerable are you?

AE Not at all. We're ready for next gen, we're very close to our publisher, and we're market leaders – together with Sony London – in social games. I don't think it's going away. I think there's really something in making these games for more people. We try to make games that include everyone in the house at the same time – we're trying to make them a more social experience.

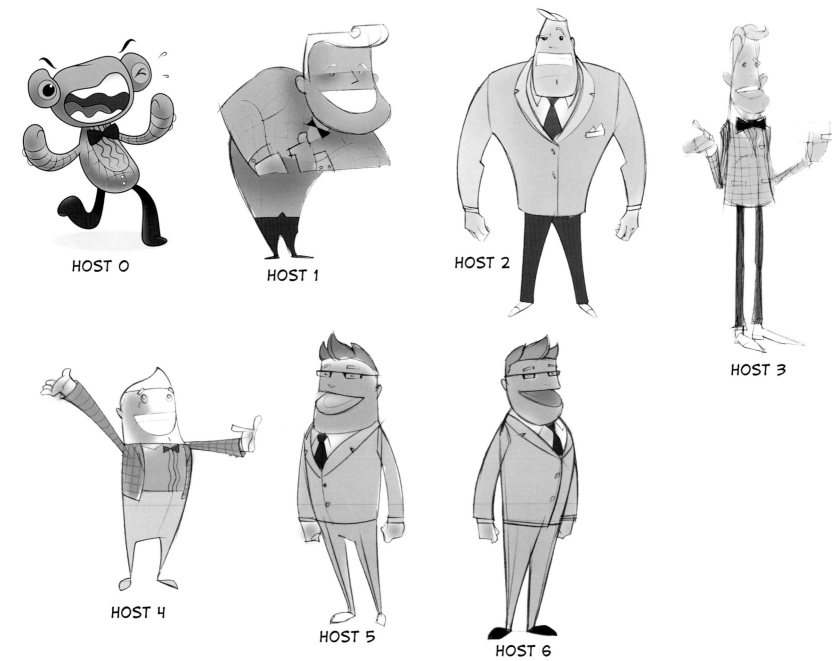

HOST 0

HOST 1

HOST 2

HOST 3

HOST 4

HOST 5

HOST 6

make a quiz game out of them?' So Sony approached us. Our first thought was 'well, quiz games, they're a bit dry, not a lot of fun.' But then we thought some more: if you did a good treatment out of it, it could really work. We had the thought of putting buzzers in the box, because we'd seen *Singstar*. [Reaches for a *Singstar* box from the shelf behind him.] You can see what this is from the other side of the store; from a mass-market point of view, people understand it. Similarly, we thought you could put four buzzers in a box. We mocked up the blister pack to show Sony, thinking that they'd say no because it was too expensive, but they thought it might be quite fun – a quiz game, set in a TV studio. And we certainly added something to the idea of a quiz show based on music clips.

When Sony first got the prototype buzzers, I'm told they tried it out at an internal party and there were people around it all night. It was a really easy fun, cool thing to do. So it started off being a fairly small project and it became apparent that it might be something that would sell more widely. Social games were getting bigger, *Singstar* and *EyeToy* were really selling, so Sony knew better than anyone else how to promote and present these social games and they were getting to these new buyers. Momentum for this kind of play was really building within Sony.

AE It's important to note that when Sony came to us, the current implementation was a board game on a TV screen, and we just thought it didn't work.

They came to you simply with the idea of a quiz game?

AE Here's a thousand questions, here's a thousand clips – what would you do with them? We came up with the *Buzz* format.

DA That's what Sony does. I don't think that's an unusual scenario. They might say to driving developers, 'we're looking at doing an off-road driving game.'

AE *DJ* [a previous project] started in much the same way.

DA Someone [at Sony] said, 'we'd like to do a game that involved house music – that seems to be popular.' I think as a designer it really helps to have some direction. Starting from a completely blank sheet of paper is tough.

At this point was Relentless already dedicated to this new kind of social gaming?

AE We didn't wake up one day and decide it; it just happened. We decided we weren't even going to think about doing a driving or fighting or football game, because why would we want to compete with those already hugely established studios. I thought there were loads of games you could do like this. Plus, it's a game type I thought we could do well in.

Why are they all English? *Singstar*, *EyeToy*, *Buzz*?

DA *Buzz* isn't being sold in America yet. I think America is more hardcore in its gamers and the people making games. I don't want to generalize too much, but the more hardcore games seem to sell well in America.

AE The density of PlayStation in the UK is pretty high compared with in the USA. There are a lot of people in the USA, but there's a similar number of PS2s. I think it has turned out that a broader spectrum of people in the UK have contact with PlayStation, which means that things like *Singstar* appeal.

DA It was interesting that in our green-light meeting for *Buzz*, Ray Maguire, the guy running Sony UK, said, 'when this releases, I need to get it into the Argos catalogue.' This wasn't about being on the shelves of Game or specialist shops so much; he wanted it to be in the Argos catalogue and on the shelves of Wal-Mart. Sony understands how to reach a wider market.

AE The difference is – and it's a double-edged sword – there are the three territories that each act independently. Microsoft is an American company with global reach; Nintendo is a Japanese company with global reach; whereas Sony Europe gets to do European stuff.

We have a fair understanding of the UK market and, by extension, Australia. We do spectacularly well there. So far, the USA and Japan haven't really picked up on this genre at all. They're very hardcore markets. I think Nintendo is thinking very hard about the social and non-gamer market. Sony Europe understands that market more than anyone.

DA The individuals who sit in their marketing department are not videogame people, and that's really important.

How important is the bespoke controller for the social game?

AE Paramount. I think you could have shipped a quiz game without a buzzer, but you don't go from the peripheral back – you go from the software challenge out. We thought you can't really do a quiz game with two people. The demographic we're going for isn't going to have a multi-tap.

So the first development challenge was to allow for enough players?

AE Yes. The buzzer was about 'how do we get four people playing this game?'

DA We came out in October, exactly so that Ray could hit his Argos catalogue as planned. Ray says, 'we've sold PlayStations to all of the teenagers now, even to a lot of the mums and dads, so now we want the products we can sell to different people.' That's what they're looking for. The first thought was, how much fun will two players be? So the buzzers came about to enable this group playing, but also to differentiate *Buzz* from the other quiz games.

RELENTLESS SOFTWARE

It was the accessibility argument that we put to Sony: first, most non-gamers are scared of a DualShock controller; second, it is four players straight out of the box. Everyone's seen those big red buttons on TV shows. Quiz shows are all about them.

How was that specifically presented to Sony? This was a radical idea with an obviously pretty high risk attached to it. Was this a big Power-Point presentation to the producer?

DA Well, Sony knew us. We were talking to Kevin McSherry, who was the producer on the quiz product, about setting the game in a TV studio. I was a little reticent, as I didn't think they'd go for it – mainly because of the cost. When I said, 'what you really want to do is stick buzzers in the box', he turned to me and said, 'I wish I'd thought of that.' Which was a really humble reaction.

There was no question that the idea was exciting and that buzzers would make a better product, but at the time it was a small product with maybe 50–100,000 sales forecast. So for maybe three or four months we were developing the game as if the buzzers might happen, or might not. We were developing rounds and seeing which ones would work with them and which ones wouldn't, just in case.

Sony handled all of the buzzer peripheral development. We did some initial sketches to show them what we were thinking, but they did all the development. The big difference between our initial prototype and theirs was that ours was a buzzer that you would have on a table, and they quite rightly thought you would need one you could hold in one hand. All they said from a design point of view was, 'what do you need?' We said, 'four buttons and a buzzer.'

That lit up?

DA We didn't specify that. We said we could do more with the gameplay if it did light up, but in truth we weren't able to use it as much as we'd liked. People don't look at the buzzers while they're playing. We had some rounds that

were based around people hitting the buzzer when it lit up, but of course no-one was looking.

It's one of the most satisfying things about it, though.

DA Sure. We had a lot of ideas around using it. One of them was that someone was nominated by the buzzer flashing, and others would guess who it was. But of course, everyone in the room could see it flashing, or even if it was hidden, they'd see someone's face reflecting red.

I think at one point Sony was a little bit worried that people would just say that there's nothing there that a standard controller can't do. I remember IGN's preview said that, 'you can do all of this with a DualShock.' *Singstar* mics and *EyeToy* cameras offer new tech to PlayStation. *Buzz* buzzers don't.

That must have been incredibly frustrating.

DA Yes. I mean, this wasn't designed as a leg-up on existing input devices.

It's all in the context…

DA Yes. I was initially worried, but if you think that a Dual-Shock can do the same thing, technically, you're right – but in practice…

So what were the other reservations, other than cost?

DA Retail. The game takes up a lot of shelf space. Thankfully, *Singstar* had already gone in with a blister pack the same size, so the foundations were laid. But if you look at *Singstar* or *Buzz* across a store without the peripherals, you just don't get it. You can't understand what it is with the front of a DVD box. Another problem is that a lot of retailers can't put it out on the shelves because it just gets stolen, so you have to make dummy boxes for that purpose. The tax involved in making a plastic blister pack rather than a cardboard box is also pretty heavy, so there is a whole set of

problems with making something a little more off the wall. It takes six weeks to get the packs from China where they're made, to the UK. A lot of games publishing is done on a just-in-time basis, but you can't do that when you have a six-week delay. This means someone has to take an enormous bet on that, and if you get it wrong, you're throwing away a lot more than it costs to make a DVD. Someone, somewhere, down the line had to sign a purchase order for more than a million buzzers.

We also had to do some unexpected things, like write software that allows the production line in China to test them. So somewhere in China, the operator is there testing all the buttons. I think the first run was 1.2 million. Not only is that a big purchase order, but also a massive manufacturing job. Someone told me they had about a hundred people manufacturing the buzzers in China. You start to realize that our contribution is just a small element – even in money terms, it's really small. What they have found though, is that the price point tends to stick. There's a perceived value in the buzzers that stops it eroding.

Andy was talking about Relentless making software that has some permanence. *Buzz* in itself could almost be a platform for any number of quizzes.

DA It's the type of product where you can come up with different scenarios without cheating anyone. We're fortunate to be in that position. You can start to see how downloadable content might work for things like PS3. You can see how people might download 'quiz of the week' or whatever for a small amount of money. There's a lot of life in it.

So let's talk about the process.

DA We decided we were going to set *Buzz* in a TV studio. We liked *Parappa* and *Katamari* [see pages 120–27]. We liked the kind of art style, and our initial art style was based on that kind of feel. It was still a quiz show, but it was very off the wall. We had a new producer on it, and a few months in he just turned to us and said 'you know what? I think this art style's rubbish.' And he was right. We were supposed to be making Saturday night TV-type format, not referencing some obscure Japanese cartoon that only you and your mates know about. So ditch the inflatable horse and how about we have an Elvis!

So what led you down that path in the first place?

DA If you're part of the *Katamari* club, it's easy to get drawn into that. We were probably trying to make something that our peers might think us clever for aping. It was good art – it just wasn't right. So we took a step back and set the game in a more traditional TV studio. That's helpful because you don't have to invent it.

In terms of characters, we went for a Muppet style with caricatures of different celebrities. We focus-tested them on non-videogame people, and they all preferred to have more realistic-looking people, not ones who looked like Muppets. A strange side effect of that was that Buzz himself stayed pretty much as a Muppet, while the contestants all became more human. It's good for lip-synching though. Some of our pop stereotypes were too close to who they were supposed to be. We had someone in a Union Jack dress and the legal people said we'd need to tone it down or Geri Halliwell would be asking us for money. But by making them stereotypes they become easier to animate, and members of the family go for their favourites. Dad *will* want to be Elvis.

What was the approach to designing the games?

DA We storyboarded different rounds. After evaluating them and making prototypes, we generally found anything at all complicated was rejected. Anything relying on reaction speed didn't work, because then Gran can't play. Anything relying on reading instructions didn't work – thus, the titles became very important. If I say 'pass the bomb' you've got some idea what the game will be. 'Sabotage' was a round that didn't make it.

Buzz is all about off-screen interaction. It's not about how well you're getting on with the game; it's about how you're getting on in the room. We try to make all the questions be answerable by three out of four of the players. We're tying to give everyone the chance to interact. In 'pass the bomb', if you've got it and it explodes, you don't blame the game for making it do that – you blame the person who just passed it to you.

Someone said to me recently, 'why don't we make a kind of Mario-kart game with little steering wheels?' But that relies on some kind of specific gameplay skill to play. We try hard to avoid that; it's a good leveller. With *Buzz*, people might know different amounts about music, but it doesn't matter how much they know about PlayStation. In terms of next-gen, more polygons don't add a great deal to *Buzz*. The big development for us is going to be moving online. To me, online sofa versus sofa is a lot more exciting than online individuals playing against individuals. But social games are only just beginning. There are loads we got wrong in *Buzz* in the beginning.

Like what?

DA Well, no-one knows that you have to push the buzzer after you finish a round. The game sits there waiting and coughing and telling you to push the buzzer, which we thought was really clever. But of course, no-one's listening because they're all getting a drink or whatever and they miss it. All I needed to do was put a little bar there saying 'push the buzzer' – but I live and learn.

Are there any areas you're looking to develop in the forthcoming versions of the game?

Mainly the downloads. The film I see in my head has *Buzz* moving from terrestrial to digital and the player suddenly has access to all this new content.

I'm interested to know if you have any lessons to share, ones that aren't covered by the way you work at Relentless?

DA At EA you have very good practices. One of the things I did was to run usability testing. I was demoing *Dungeon Keeper 2* at E3 on the show floor. At one point in it, you can go first-person. Without question, the thing that got the most reaction was this honeycomb thing where you become a fly and fly around. To me, it was just a filter, but it was written about everywhere. So as designer, you learn that the things you thought were important are the things people often don't get. I worked on a version of *Theme Park* where no-one understood that you could change the levels of the track, so people were making these totally flat roller-coasters.

These episodes made me realize that the way you think a game is going to be played rarely is the way it will be played. It's not a crime to be simple. With *Buzz*, people build their own experiences around it. We let other people have fun with our basic framework.

AE My first job was making chess programs; you can still buy a chess program that I had some involvement in, and I think that's brilliant. Games can sell for a long time; they don't have to be these short-lifespan products. Two months after the release of *Buzz* and we'd just gone back up to number three in the PS2 chart. I just hate the idea that you'd put four years of your life into a product that might only have two months to sell.

One of my old bosses said, 'if it takes two years to make a videogame, and you're in the industry for 20 years until you get so senior you're out of creative production, then that's ten games – ten chances to get a number-one hit.' That doesn't sound like many to me. So my philosophy is to throw more darts.

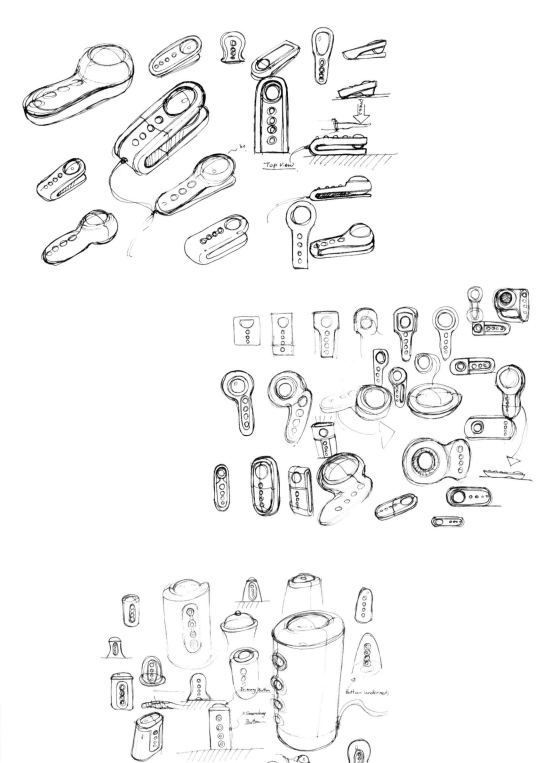

this spread From a focused design brief of 'four buttons and a buzzer' a wide variety of options was considered before the final one-handed peripheral was finalized. One of the most important elements of the entire package, it has since been used as a control mechanism in non-*Quiz* titles.

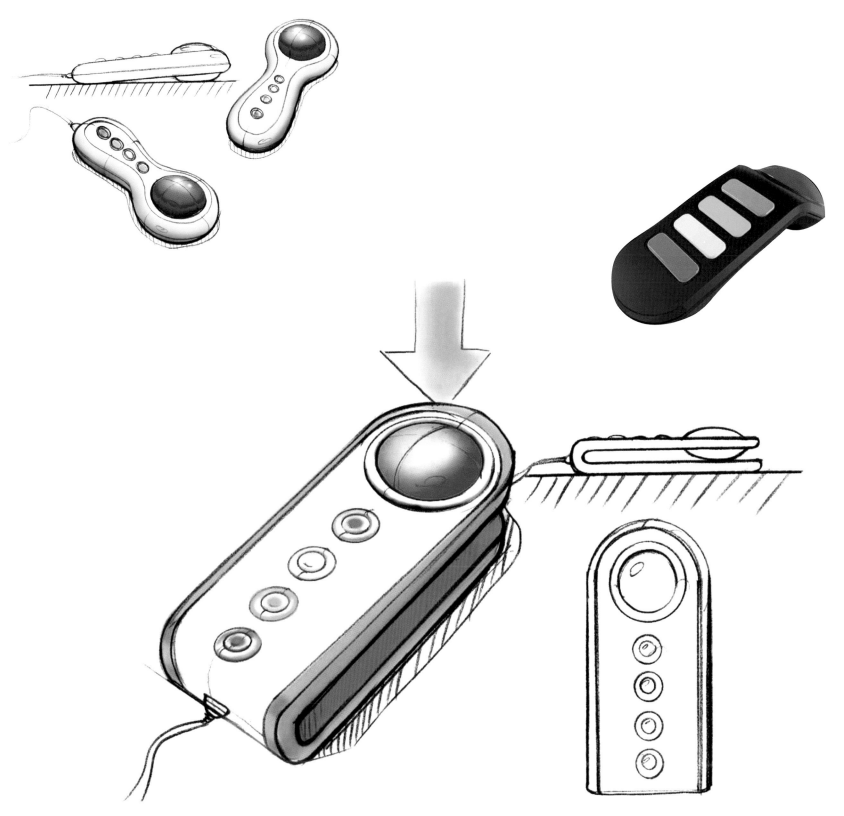

118

1

2

3

4

5

clockwise from top left
1 Keita Takahashi.
2 Building housing Takahashi's studio in Yokohama.
3 Takahashi's desk.
4 & 5 Studio stress-relieving devices.

KEITA TAKAHASHI

LOCATION

Yokohama, Japan

STAFF

13

KEY TITLES

We ♥ Katamari (2005)

Katamari Damacy (2004)

SELECTED AWARDS

Game Developers Choice Awards, Excellence in Game Design, *Katamari Damacy* (2005)

Gold Prize, Japanese Industrial Design Promotion Awards, *Katamari Damacy* (2004)

IT SEEMED AS IF HE CAME OUT OF NOWHERE. SUDDENLY IN 2004, everyone who cared about games was talking about an obscure PS2 title that wasn't even available in Europe. The word-of-mouth on Keita Takahashi's breakthrough title, the sublimely silly *Katamari Damacy*, was extraordinary. In a matter of months, Takahashi had become symbolic of everything that could be in modern game design. Without volunteering, he had become a poster child for innovation, playfulness and unadulterated freedom in game design.

Playing, or even just watching, *Katamari*, it's not difficult to see why. Concerned with a prince who needs to reinstate the stars and planets to the cosmos (after his father accidentally destroys them), it's a disarmingly charming game. The simple gameplay concept, of rolling around a 'Katamari' (a large sticky ball) to which everything adheres was instantly accessible. Combined with the highly stylized art design and Tokyo-pop soundtrack, the game throbbed with an individuality seldom seen in a major console title.

Takahashi became widely fêted, receiving ovations simply for turning up at developer conferences around the world. Curiously, the man himself has always seemed genuinely confused (possibly a little bemused?) by the global attention.

This interview took place through translation, and over email.

I'm interested to know how game ideas emerge for you. For example, are they visual? Are they control-based?

As you know, I currently work in the game industry. If the whole industry and my daily work was to be repetitive, following the same routines every day, I think it would be normal to start seeking for excitement such as popping out for a drink with someone you recently met at a place you have never visited before. In other words, trying to break a daily routine is definitely one of the starting points for me when looking for new ideas.

However, I see concepts being a true reflection of what you want to make, which takes into account the trends that can be found at the time. Ideas are random thoughts that suddenly pop up, and so I definitely feel concepts are more important.

Although somewhat limited in my areas of interests, I think I became rather sensitive to trends while studying at university. Such information is usually filtered through my brain, which usually results in an end product that can only be decoded and understood by myself. Because of that, it was a surprise to see that the world of *Katamari* was accepted well and understood by everyone at the time.

Looking back, I don't think the world has changed much in terms of environmental issues. The question I always had was 'what would be my role on this planet regarding this issue?' I think this theme was reflected in *Katamari* without me noticing it at the time.

I feel this idea was implemented in the game to express doubts about market-driven mass production and consumption. I suppose living in Japan is a decisive factor, as there are too many products on the market. I can't imagine coming up with some of the ideas I had if I were living in some discreet location with access to the world of nature.

I'd say my ideas are visual. An image becomes visible in my head when something crops up, although it is rather faint at first. It is difficult to explain how such an idea materializes, since we are talking about visual ideas becoming a proper shape or piece.

Due to the difficulty of explaining the visuals in my head, I prefer to work in small groups when developing an idea. Passing on information by writing is useful when it comes to communicating facts objectively, but it is not ideal when trying to pass on concepts and detail to someone else.

Therefore, I usually minimize the number of documents I create and prefer to talk to anyone in charge using visual illustrations when required to get any ideas moving. This is an old-fashioned, non-productive method that gives a headache to the management, I suppose.

How do you evaluate these ideas?

That is rather difficult to answer. A sort of criteria definitely exists within me, but I cannot figure out how exactly to put it into context.

What usually happens is the following. When I come up with an idea that feels interesting, I usually share the idea with someone and talk it over. But I have to admit, I normally choose who I speak to first and that person is usually someone I know who will understand my philosophy. The funny thing is, what I feel as being interesting as an idea is usually accepted by that person as well. Talking to someone who can give you feedback definitely helps to start with. It was quite easy with *Katamari*, but what I'm doing at the moment is not so easy. The project has been going on for a while, but I still don't feel my idea and concept has been fully understood by everyone just yet. I'm sure I'll get there in the end, though.

You seem to embrace a far wider set of cultural references than most videogame-makers. You've also said that you don't see yourself as a game designer, which I can wholly understand. How does your game-making intersect with the rest of your creative life? For example, do you consciously see how your games might inform your sculptural work and vice versa?

That's a difficult question! This is nothing to do with me personally, but a game called *Mushi King* was a big hit in Japan recently. It was a beetle-fighting game for boys – in particular. Considering the Japanese market, it was not surprising that the sales of real beetles went up as well at the time.

I think the promotion side of the industry has created a good trend recently by not limiting a new title to just being a game. In other words, we tend to see more intellectual properties moving into a different area such as character figures or movies. However, if the question is to remain solely on the concepts and expressions of a certain title influencing different areas of the business world, I'd say 'no' at this time. The reason is simple. I feel the original fun of games in general has lost its appeal compared to the heyday. Games with original ideas have been on the decline and the graphic-heavy titles are now the main focal point. I fully appreciate this fact is tied in with technological improvements, but I still feel that this is not the only talking point for videogames.

The world of videogames can create environments and rules that cannot occur in the real world. Videogames can create a different approach to what is available in the world. Conversely, if the creative approaches and concepts created by the game industry could be applied in the real world, I'm sure the world would be a more peaceful place. Perhaps I've digressed too much, but let's hope that one day a title will appear that will positively influence the world we live in.

You've talked a lot about the influences on your work from other arts and media. Do you think it's helpful when the hardware itself becomes a clear influence on the design? I remember you didn't feel that about the Wii at first. I was wondering if your thoughts had changed?

I have to admit that I don't play videogames too much, so it is difficult for me to answer the question in terms of the industry as a whole – although I can share some of my personal opinions in this case. On a personal note, anything that is abnormal in terms of its design interests me. For example, whenever I see a picture that is original in its own right, I tend to see my limitation for expressing my ideas and feel encouraged to become more flexible.

Also the clothes the so-called *obachan* (Japanese middle-aged ladies) wear is always eye-catching. I'm quite sure a minor tweak in the design would make it a Paris Collection (design week) contender. Their freedom of mind is reflected in the colour co-ordination of their clothes. It is interesting to see them on the street, although some designs and colours do make me laugh from time to time.

Also, when playing with my sister's children, I notice they tend to react in ways I can't think in any more. For them, everything is a playground, hiding behind advertisement boards and using anything on the roadside for fun. Everything is a new creation for them, which comes naturally without thinking. It seems like we can't stop ourselves from getting old.

I feel that knowing the technical limits of a console is a necessity, but not too important in a sense. Why do I feel that way? Well, to be honest with you, I joined the company without too much knowledge of PCs. However, I still managed to contribute in creating a game on what was my first assignment at the time, so I don't see being technical as always a necessity.

Having said that, you will get a blank face from the programmers once in a while when talking to them of your idea and the project might slow down, so studying as you go should be good enough in my opinion. At the end of the day, you need to know what you want to make and work your way towards making that happen, so I don't think we can simply say whether knowing the hardware helps or not.

I think the Wii is good fun. The console entrance has been left wide open for everyone and I can see it being accepted by a wide audience in a short period of time. However, I think working for the industry has decreased the fun for me slightly because of its originality.

One of the highlights of the Wii is the motion sensor enabling you to use your whole body to play a game. Moving your body is fun as it is, and one piece of advice from me is to imagine the movement of your muscles and bones as you move them and this alone should increase the fun of Wii just a bit more.

However, on a very personal point of view as a developer, highlighting too much of the 'use your body to play the game' approach can to some degree look like denying videogaming's past as a whole. I don't know how to pass on

my thoughts on this issue but I just can't help feeling that everything is not right somehow.

Using your body is good exercise and being able to play tennis and bowling virtually in such an accessible way is something Nintendo should be proud of. However, I'm not sure if moving your body according to the gameplay is the same as having your body moved by a certain gimmick within, let's say, an action game when something comes out of the blue on the screen.

I feel that gaming experience is made up from the imaginary and creative brain a player holds as well. What's fun is fun, but getting that extra tension and fun feel from a game is down to the creative side and the game. Maybe I'm being too conservative, but with the number of titles on the decrease in terms of originality and creativity, I do feel the danger of moving into the easy approach Wii has provided us with.

Please don't get me wrong; the Wii itself is definitely fun as a console, but I'm not totally convinced with the console at this stage.

Developers around the world clearly see your work as inspirational, not just in and of itself, but because you represent a kind of creative freedom that few experience. What's the best advice you can give creative people?

The simple advice from me is, don't try to become like me! What's the point of having similar games created by similar-thinking people? We don't want to see the same – or nearly the same – titles lining up on the shelves do we? But my advice is, don't be afraid to express your ideas and be yourself! Let's face it, surely there can't be too many people who want to become like me anyway!

How do you (physically) arrange your work studio to be as good as it can be for you? What things are important?

My ideal workplace would be an open-air environment with plenty of sunshine. It would be good fun to have your desk

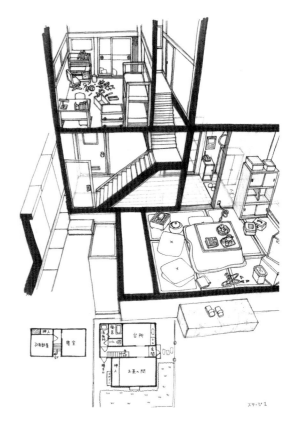

surrounded by a flock of sheep, for example, or hummingbirds stopping by to perch on your monitor for a while. Since it's in the open air, we would have to stop working when it rains, which could result in your project being delayed. Even so, I'm sure we would see excellent-quality titles popping up now and then.

Well, back to reality then. I don't have too much of a preference, but I just can't stand partitions. Some people say that productivity increases as people can concentrate more, but I don't see that. You already have a PC monitor in front of you, which pretty much keeps you tied up during the day while at your desk. Having a partition around it simply reduces the opportunity to have a quick conversation with other people in the office.

124

Maybe the partition layout is useful for routine work where one knows the exact requirements, but it is definitely not for me. Communication is important, not just for myself but for my colleagues as well. Open layout is definitely the keyword for me.

Is there a particular place or time when you find you're able to be more creative?

Not really. New ideas tend to pop up while I'm having a walk or while travelling on the train, and so on. I definitely cannot come up with anything when I'm stuck in one place thinking about one thing only.

When I need to come up with something, I'll just say to myself, let's start thinking, and out of the blue something will drop into my head if it's a good day. Then by talking to someone about the initial idea, the idea starts to become more real and gradually takes shape.

Can you take me through a typical day in the life of the development of a project?

I usually arrive in the office around 10 in the morning and check my emails to start with. Then I'll browse the Internet for news on macs and other electronic gadgets before starting to work properly at around 10.30. After replying to emails and talking over new ideas with the team, it's quite normal for the workday to end at about 11 in the evening. Then I'll start finishing off and will start to make my way home and usually go to bed at 2 in the morning.

I know that you've expressed a will to work in other forms, specifically playgrounds. Do you think that working in other mediums would benefit all game designers?

Yes, I definitely think that's important. Some people say that it will add extra value to the games you create by knowing the outside world but for me, it's more simple. My philosophy is to do whatever you want to do when you want to.

What's the point in limiting yourself to what you're working on when you never know how you will feel about your job when you wake up the next morning.

Some people might continue in the same industry throughout their working career, whereas some may come up with something new at some stage. In that sense, I don't see why people who have never touched the world of videogames couldn't try to make one and open up the possibility of the industry as a whole. On a personal note, it will be ideal for me if I can keep on creating new games as well as designing T-shirts and playgrounds, for example. I'm sure this will open up the possibilities for making the whole industry more active and creative by blending their cultures and ways of thinking.

Finally, I'd like to get some of your broader thoughts about play and how it relates to what you do. These questions are intentionally open to allow you some space to answer as broadly as you like.

I believe videogames are something that are there to surprise the players. A simple 'wow' is the phrase I would like to hear when someone is playing. Some reactions or feedback we receive concern things that we would never have thought of, and these are valuable to us.

I always have some long-term beliefs in myself, a vision that spans the next 10, 20 years or so. Things I made while at university, and the recent *Katamari*, are a reflection of what I saw of the world in my everyday life as well. Using something that is around you every day makes it easier for

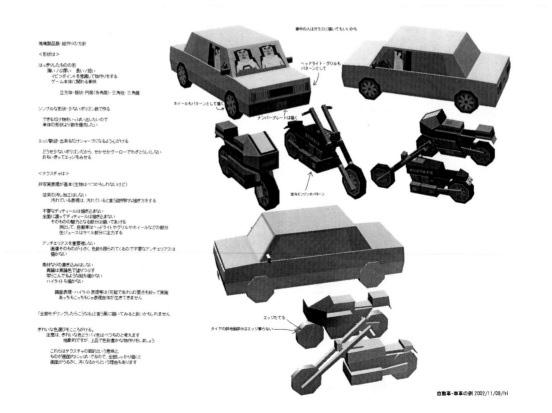

below The prince, player avatar and hero of the *Katamari* series of games.

125

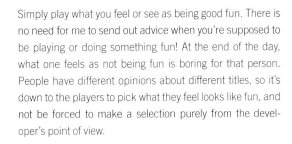

people to evaluate and hopefully understand my work. It's normal for us to see things differently despite looking at the same things. I feel this difference is what makes the world a more flexible place. I try to implement both aspects from both ends in my games, as well as adding something humorous and shocking to the users that can be created only in the world of videogames.

It is difficult to pass on my message to the players through the games completely, but hopefully someone out there will be able to catch and understand some of the message I'm trying to get across. But at the end of the day, I'm the one who wants to be impressed the most from what I make. I'm making the game for myself to a degree.

What are your videogames for? What would you advise anyone who wanted to make them?

Creating or developing a videogame doesn't mean you will become famous and get well paid or get invited for excellent meals everyday. I suppose it depends on the person, but even getting a date could be a problem sometimes! But it is a job where you have the freedom to express yourself, so one mission is to create something that will make someone surprised and make them want to play the game even more.

However, we do need electricity to get the console going to start with, so every gamer will need to be careful how we use electricity. I'm sure it will be beneficial for everyone in the long term as well! Maybe I've digressed too much yet again, but let's be friendly to the environment.

What advice would you give to someone who wanted to play them?

Simply play what you feel or see as being good fun. There is no need for me to send out advice when you're supposed to be playing or doing something fun! At the end of the day, what one feels as not being fun is boring for that person. People have different opinions about different titles, so it's down to the players to pick what they feel looks like fun, and not be forced to make a selection purely from the developer's point of view.

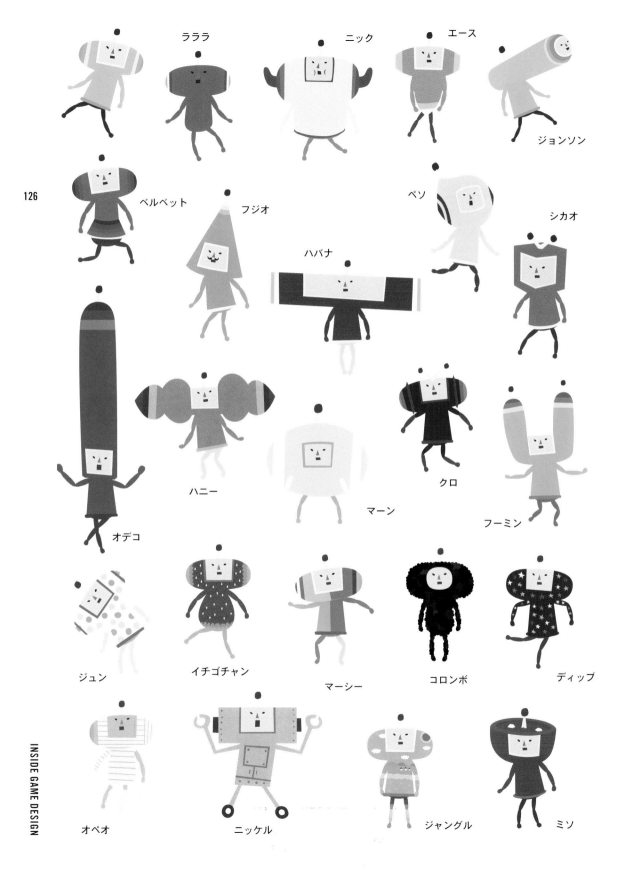

ラララ

ニック

エース

ジョンソン

ベルベット

フジオ

ハバナ

ペソ

シカオ

オデコ

ハニー

マーン

クロ

フーミン

ジュン

イチゴチャン

マーシー

コロンボ

ディップ

オペオ

ニッケル

ジャングル

ミソ

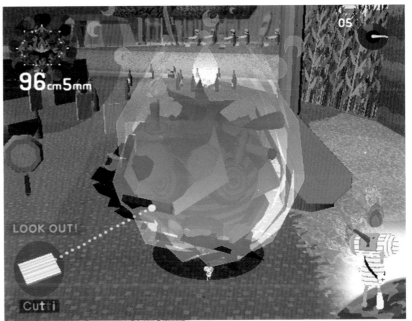

KEITA TAKAHASHI

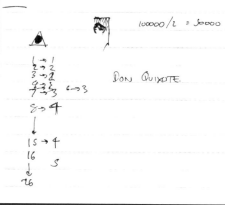

29 = SIR.

A GAME WHERE YOU CONTROL 2 UNITS
AT ONCE WITH ~~JOYSTICK~~ THUMBSTICK.

100000/2 = 50000

1 → 1
2 → 2
3 → 2
4,7,8,3 6 → 3
8 → 4

15 → 4
16   5

26

DON QUIXOTE.

clockwise from top left
1 Torpex coder Jamie Fristrom's working habitat.
2 Fristrom.
3 The very beginning – *Schizoid* began with this scrap of paper.

TORPEX GAMES

www.torpexgames.com
www.gamedevblog.com

LOCATION
Various, USA

STAFF
2–6

KEY TITLE
Schizoid (working title) (2007)

TORPEX IS AN UNUSUAL START-UP. LIKE FREE RADICAL IN THE UK (see pages 28–39), it's a company formed from alumni of a great film-licence videogame. *Spider-Man 2*, like *Goldeneye* before it, demonstrated that licences don't have to be cynical cash-ins. President Bill Dugan was executive producer on *Spider-Man 2* and estimates the games he has worked on have grossed $200 million worldwide. Partner and technical director Jamie Fristrom invented the acclaimed swinging mechanic for *Spider-Man 2* and blogs a wonderfully detailed insight into game development on his site (www.gamedevblog.com). Finally, for their new project they are collaborating with Richard Garfield and Skaff Elias, two of the most important designers in trading-card games.

Dugan and Fristrom were riding high on the global critical and commercial success of *Spider-Man 2* when they decided to move from Los Angeles to start a new company. There is thus only one sensible question with which to start this interview with Fristrom…

You just relocated to Seattle from directing what will probably be one of the biggest console releases of 2007. Why?

Excellent question. They made me one of two creative directors on *Spider-Man 3*, so I'd have to be nuts to give up a plum job like that, right?

It's what a lot of people might be thinking…

Will Wright is one of my heroes. One thing he said once was something along the lines of – he'd rather parachute in on completely new territory than continue to explore nearby ground in an old territory. That's why he went on to make *The Sims* instead of *Sim City 3000*; that's why he went on to *Spore* instead of the *Sims 2*. So we'd already done something revolutionary with *Spider-Man 2*, but *Spider-Man 3* was going to be more of an evolution than a revolution. We did come up with some cool stuff, and I think it's going to be a good game, but I wasn't as passionate about it as *Spidey 2*.

Add to that, I always wanted to try the entrepreneur thing. My contract with Activision came to an end, and I decided it was time to try something new. I guess *Spidey 3* and our game – which we're still looking for a name for, the working title right now is 'Schizoid' – will have shipped by the time your readers see this, so they'll have a perspective that I don't at the moment…

So this new territory you wanted to explore wasn't just design territory – it was entrepreneurial too? Did you have a clear sense of what you wanted to make?

I was hoping you'd ask that. No – we had no idea what we wanted to make.

None at all?

Another one of my heroes is Jim Collins, author of *Built to Last*, a book on managing businesses. He mentions that a lot of great companies – Hewlett Packard, Sony, 3M, the list goes on – didn't know what they'd do. They just knew they wanted to start a company and had vision for what kind of company it would be.

So you had a vision?

Bill and I knew we wanted to make great, addictive, innovative games, but didn't know what they'd be.

Did you know what people would play them on?

Nope. We figured since we were console guys a console deal was the most likely thing we'd be able to find.

So that was a practical rather than a conceptual consideration?

Yes.

129

So you start a games company. I know you had some ideas you were kicking around…

We looked into a lot of stuff: mobile, serious, casual downloadable on PC, handheld.

Am I right in thinking Torpex = Jamie and Bill at this point?

Yes. Bill founded the company with another idea in mind (which we're not ready to unveil yet) a year before I joined.

Can we unpack the ideas stage for a while? I'm interested in how these memes appear to you.

The 'where do you get your ideas?' thing?

No, the 'what do your ideas look like?' thing.

A lot of times when you join a company you can explicitly list intellectual property that you consider 'yours' just so there are no disagreements later about whether that idea you came up with was your own or your new company's, especially in teams. This may be off-topic. But those times are when my game ideas get crystallized. I scour my hard drive and my notes, and anything I've ever thought of gets listed.

Can you give an example of what a note might contain? Are we talking 'Die Hard on the Moon'-type pitches?

At the most nebulous, I might email myself with a sentence or two to jog my memory. Most of them are documents, maybe a few thousand words, on my hard drive. Some of them I make into board games, and a few of them I actually take the effort to write some code and create rough prototypes for.

A couple of thousand words? That's the kind of length of an initial idea note for you?

This one – an idea for a *Batman* game that would take place entirely within Arkham Asylum – is 1,000 words. I wrote it just for fun as I figured it would never get made, because I would never be in a position to get those kinds of rights. Here's an excerpt:

The rest of the game is similar to a third-person three-dimensional Castlevania *or* Metroid. *Batman must explore the creepy Arkham Asylum, part-mansion, part-castle, part-insane asylum, trying to recover the tools from his utility belt: batarangs and other weapons, a personal digital assistant and software that gives him clues, first-aid kits, and various kinds of grappling hooks – one that allows him to go straight up wherever there is a wooden ceiling; one that allows him to swing across chasms where there are useful hooks; and one that allows him to zipline down to depths that would otherwise kill him. These allow him to open up new areas of the asylum, previously unavailable.*

In hindsight, it's not exactly 'parachuting onto new territory.' Guess I just like *Batman*…

So this description describes the game in very broad terms. There's a shared understanding of Batman and the aesthetic decisions that will probably follow that licence. Are the systemic ideas at this point pretty much described as you have here in terms of detail?

Yes, it doesn't get any more specific than that, unless I make a board game or prototype.

Are they always textual, these initial sketches?

Almost always pure text. One exception (another game that will probably never get made) was I wanted to combine *Spider-Man*'s swinging mechanic with a shooting game. I guess like *Bionic Commando* but in 3D. I did some level design for that in Google Sketchup.

I think I remember you mentioning that as a Wii title.

It would be really interesting to try a swinging mechanic on the Wii. With some ideas, you just know they're cool before you even try them. Most you don't.

Before committing these things to paper, how do you experience them? I don't mean this to sound as hippy as it reads, but are these imaginative leaps, things you can see? It feels as if these initial ideas for you really are analogous to film treatments or book proposals – but as you say, you don't know until they're made. Which is where the real detail begins.

You don't really experience them except in your head, which is why prototyping is so important.

Can we talk about *Schizoid*? Can we unpick the genesis of that a little in the face of the above?

Schizoid was a crazy idea. I have a scrap of notepaper from a game conference where I scribbled a note to myself: 'Game where you control two guys with the two sticks on the gamepad.' I then promptly forgot about that note, and was just having fun on my birthday, playing around with different game prototyping systems when I decided to give it a go and thought it was pretty fun. Because you were controlling two guys at once, I needed to make them 'orthogonal' to make the game interesting, so I made them different colours, and made the enemies different colours, so red could only kill red and blue could only kill blue. I was digging it, so I showed it to Bill, and he said, 'let's show it to [the level designers] Richard [Garfield] and Skaff [Elias].'

Richard and Skaff thought it was way too hardcore, but Richard really liked the way the different colours worked, and said, 'what about a co-op game, where each person plays one colour?' So we tried that, and that turned out to be really fun, 'just one more quarter' fun. So that became what the game is about. 'Schizoid' doesn't make much sense as a title now. I still like the name, but we're mulling over others.

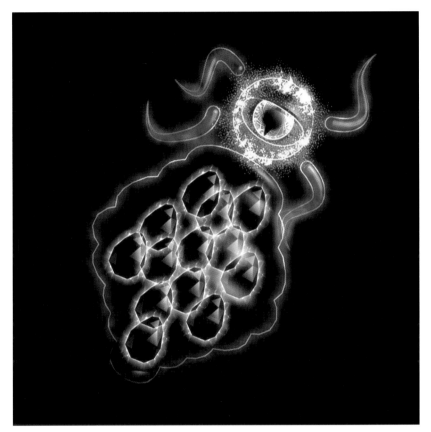

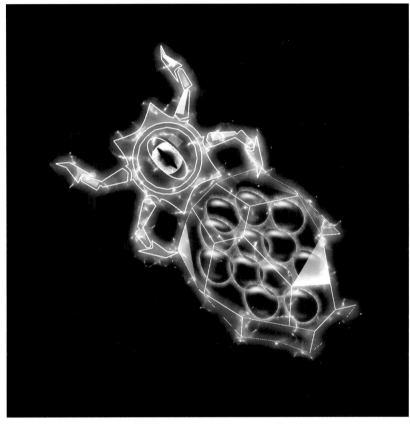

So it's only multi-player?

I've developed an AI to play your companion so you can still play single-player – or, if you're hardcore, you can play it 'Schizoid' and control both.

The schizoid concept sounds awesome.

You must be hardcore.

People rarely say that.

We all love *Gauntlet*. *Schizoid* is even more co-op than *Gauntlet*, because if your teammate lets you down you're really screwed. It may be the most co-op videogame ever.

So by this point it was 100% an Xbox Live candidate game?

'Schizoid' mode requires a gamepad with two sticks. But now that you can also play just one guy, it's possible we'll make it for the PC as well.

In terms of how you progressed the design and prototype to that point – it sounds as if you've already decided that you're making a particularly arcade-oriented title, or am I misreading you?

That's true. After the first two days I thought, 'this would fit on Xbox Live Arcade, or maybe Sony's downloadable thing.'

Were your design thoughts kind of capped by that? Presumably there comes a point early on where you start to visualize the title on a certain platform and context?

What really capped design thoughts was budget.

Because it was your own?

If we want to own the brand, we can't ask publishers for money, so we're basically asking ourselves, 'what can we do

132

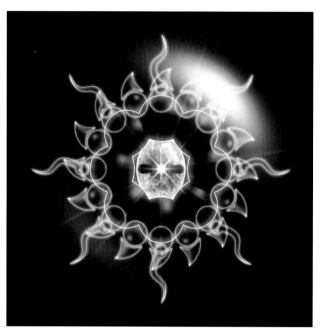

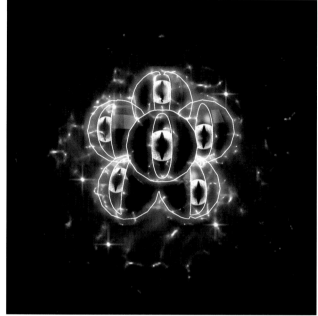

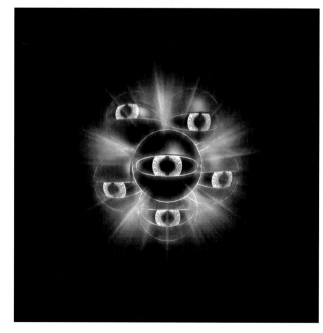

on our own dime?' The answer is an arcade-style 2D game, something with a *Geometry Wars* sort of look.

So now the prototype is in place, presumably in terms of both design and then the ongoing process, you're going to have to be really tightly planned. Can you talk a little about where you are with the project right now and what's going to happen next?

A month ago we brought an artist on, another *Spidey 2* veteran; he's been replacing my 'programmer art' with good art. He has a great system for making the enemy graphics: he plays the crap out of the game, analyzing the way the enemies behave, and then he draws an enemy that fits that behaviour. So, for example, there's a guy who darts around in random straight lines. That guy is a cloud of eyes looking in all different directions. What's next is we bring on the level designers, and Richard and Skaff have agreed to be that.

So, essentially, the core system is nailed. It now becomes about development and iteration. Theme and variations.

Yes. The game still has plenty of room to evolve, as well. Do we have power-ups? What kind of power-ups? Do we have level-warping points like *Stargate* or *Gauntlet*, or a 'Continue From Here' like a modern console game? Let's have another enemy, one that can do such-and-such. And all these cool ideas we have for improving the game exist in tension with the need to cross the t's and dot the i's, all the boring stuff you have to do to get a game out. Localize all the text to a bunch of languages; make a trial version; make sure it meets all of the console manufacturer's requirements.

Where does Torpex operate from for this part of the process? Am I right in thinking that up till now you have all been working pretty much remotely?

Yes, we're a 'Distributed Development Environment': James is in California, Richard's in Oregon, Skaff, Bill and I are in Seattle; our sound guy is in the Bay area. In the morning, we have conference calls and are very flexible about what we do on a given day.

Does being such a small team and so spread out bring a strict delineation of roles?

You know, James is actually something of a programmer. If we had any other artist, I'd have to provide the tools for him to get his art into the game. Because he's James, he just dives into the code himself. So, in a way, he's doing some of the programming. Ditto for Richard and Skaff. On the other hand, I guess there's delineation in that James is the only guy who can make decent art, and I'm the only guy who can do the network programming.

In terms of managing this process and project, it must help a lot that you're all seasoned vets.

Totally. Although it's funny – one of the things we've learned in our years of experience is that you can't really plan a game, you just have to get in there and make it, and make it as good as possible before time runs out.

I always had you down as a real planning obsessive.

One thing I'm obsessive about is doing the 'absolutely necessary' stuff before doing the 'cool' stuff. This is a constant battle – nobody wants to work on the boring necessary stuff.

What's the most important stuff to do?

Things like fixing bugs, or internationalization, or the user interface, or leader boards, or console manufacturer requirements. I think amateurs leave that stuff till last and then suffer.

I've been asked by the publisher to make sure I ask a 'what's the best advice you can give to game design students' question – have I already got the answer to that?

Well, no, because a game design student's in a special place. He's not trying to get a game to market; he's probably trying to sell a game idea to a publisher, or show off a game idea to a company that's going to give him a job. So he shouldn't work on anything boring; his game demo should be all about being cool. If, joy of joy, his demo gets green-lit, he needs to crack down and do the boring stuff.

And by 'cool' we mean.

Core gameplay. If he's got a choice between adding a power-up that might be really cool or adding a front end so you don't have to restart the game from the Windows desktop every time you want to play, he should add the power-up. Serious bugs, however, need to be fixed no matter what. It's time spent now to save time later.

This is going to sound patronizing, but my best advice for game design students would be to make games. You would not believe how many people want to be game designers who have never even tried making a game. If they can't program, maybe they can make Flash games or *Unreal* levels or *Neverwinter Nights* levels. If they can't draw, maybe they can make text adventures or rogue-likes. If they can't do either, maybe board games or card games or D&D [Dungeons and Dragons] modules. But make some games – and have people play them.

this page

1 An early build made almost entirely of programmer art.

2 Another build demonstrating programmer art particle effects.

3 The backgrounds are generated using non-linear iterated function systems.

4 The whip-like 'filament of death' power-up is added by programmer Chip Brown...

134

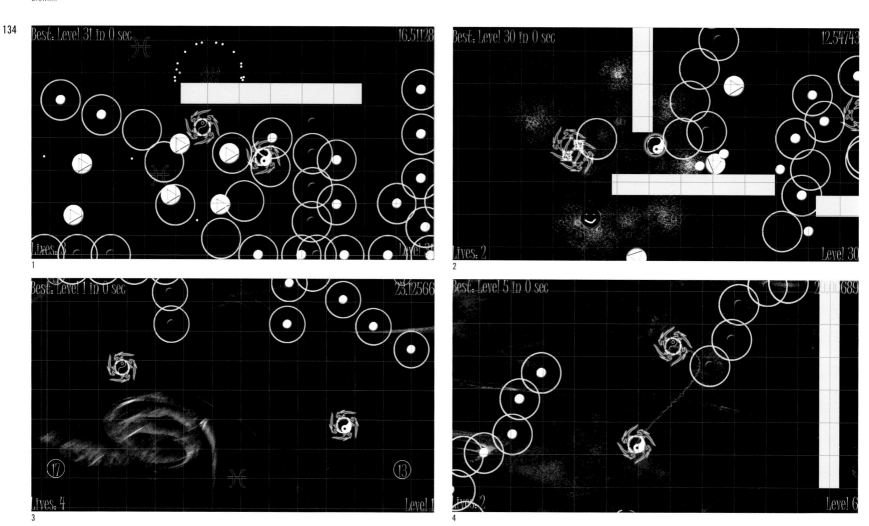

1

2

3

4

this page

5 … along with procedural lighting.

6 The art director joins the project and the 'horoscope' theme is ditched in favour of 'fire and ice'.

7 Colours are made more saturated in response to feedback that players couldn't tell the difference between fire and ice.

8 With enemy art replaced with final artwork, the grid, particle systems and backgrounds are still to be finalized.

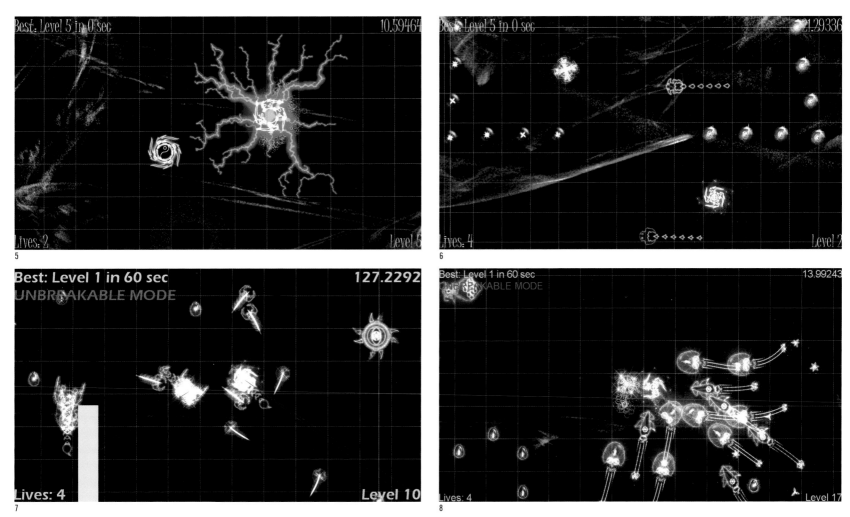

1

2

VALVE

www.valvesoftware.com

LOCATION
Bellevue, USA

STAFF
70+

KEY TITLES
Half-Life 2: Episode One (2006)
Half-Life 2 (2004)
Half-Life (1998)

SELECTED AWARDS
BAFTA, PC Game of the Year, *Half-Life 2* (2004)
AIAS. PC Game of the Year, *Half-Life 2* (2004)
PC Gamer, Best Game of All Time, *Half-Life* (1999, 2001, 2005)

VALVE, THE DEVELOPERS' DEVELOPER, HAS KEPT ITS POSITION AS one of the most progressive, interesting and innovative companies in the world over the last ten years by maintaining a strict quality-control policy over its work that few developers could afford to keep. But although it has a track record of producing brilliant games, its influence over the industry extends far further than just production. With the launch of Steam in 2002, the company made a bold step into digital distribution. Steam has largely proved to be a commercial and critical triumph, offering visibility and commercial viability to projects such as *Darwinia* and *Rag Doll Kung Fu* that would otherwise be hugely difficult to find.

Valve is a company populated in part from the active mod community. This strategy of looking for talent in less usual places and putting its investment where its instincts are has led to some unorthodox hires. Not the least of these is the team behind *Portal* – a radical new *Half-Life 2* mod, which took the Internet by storm in 2006.

Here, *Portal* designer Kim Swift gives some insight into how to get hired at Valve…

I read an interview where you talk about running a demo of *Narbacular Drop* at Valve, and 15 minutes in Gabe Newell offers you a job. Can you remember what he said?

Well, *Narbacular Drop* was our student project at DigiPen Institute of Technology, located in Redmond, WA. There were seven of us working on the project: myself, Jeep Barnett, Garret Rickey, Dave Kircher, Realm Lovejoy, Paul Graham and Scott Klintworth.

Every year, DigiPen holds a job fair for graduating seniors and brings in various game developers to take a look at student projects. A couple of people from Valve came by and took a look at *Narbacular Drop*. We must have made a good impression because they invited us to come in to their offices to demo the game for Gabe Newell and other members of Valve.

We leapt at the opportunity, while of course being extremely nervous about showing our project to some of the best and brightest in the game industry. We honestly thought we were just going in to get feedback, but as I've said before, about 15 minutes into the demonstration, Gabe quiets down the room. And to answer your question, the first words Gabe ever spoke to us were, 'so, what are you guys doing after school?' So, long story short, here we all are at Valve, making *Portal* and eager to see what the world thinks of our game.

Moving from a student development team into an established developer like Valve must have been an extraordinary experience. Did your working processes change a lot with the move into Valve? You talked in an interview about playtesting specifically being something you didn't do a lot of at college – were there other processes you gained from Valve?

It was amazing and a bit daunting all at the same, but everyone at Valve was very supportive and willing to help us adjust. Working here, I know I learn something new every day to help make me a better game developer.

One of the many things that we learned is the Valve design process. Design as a team, watch someone playtest the work, evaluate the design and rinse and repeat until we come up with something that we all can agree on is fun.

It's a very scientific-method-minded approach to design that I think is very effective. After all, what you may think is fun might not be fun for others, so what better way to find out than have others play as often as possible? It also allows us to be more objective about our own work by seeing it in context. It's very clear if something isn't working correctly, and this applies to everyone: artists, programmers and level designers alike.

Can you tell me a little about how the team works together in designing a *Portal* level? Who's involved? Is there a finely honed process you use now or are you still making discoveries about how best to do it?

138

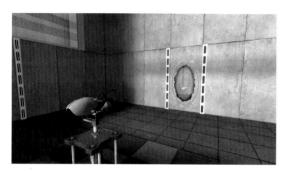

When we are ready to design a new level, all of us on the team sit down in one of the conference rooms here, caffeinated beverages in hand, and start working out our ideas on a whiteboard. Typically, we'll first decide on the purpose of the level: will this be a training room, will this be practice for a particular skill, and so on. Then using our toolbox of various gameplay elements, we'll design a room that we hope will accomplish our goal.

One of us will create a basic shell of the level with the gameplay components working, and we'll get someone to test it to see if our ideas worked. From there, we'll pass around the level, making revisions on it based on what we learn from our tests. I wish I could give you an incredible process that would blow your mind, but the methods that we find work are very practical and straightforward.

Can you tell me how you make sure that your team continues to innovate? Are there any specific things you draw upon for inspiration?

Well, I may be the talking head, but we all push one another to take things to the next level. It's definitely a group effort, and the inspiration that keeps us going is really each other.

For instance, our ever-so-excellent writers, Chet Faliszek and Erik Wolpaw, may say something that sparks Jeep to contribute, which then makes Garret add to the idea, which makes me start scrawling on the whiteboard, and so on. Having a team that can keep each other motivated and excited is incredibly important and is something I'm extremely grateful for being a part of.

Doing a little research for this, I read on your BlueCapra homepage that what you really want to be is a videogame producer. You talk about communication challenges between left- and right-brained people – specifically artists and programmers. Could you talk a little bit about how those challenges manifested during *Portal* development, and how/if they were solved? Is a little tension helpful?

I haven't looked at that webpage in about a year and a half! So, I've heard that most game companies often keep their artists and their programmers separated on a game project. I think this is a bad policy in general.

On *Portal*, we have artists, programmers and level designers in the same cabal room together to help enable better communication. Communication is a skill and skills take practice. The more opportunities artists and programmers have to better understand each other and value the other's talents, the better.

Also, another benefit of all of us watching others playtest regularly is it lets everyone stay on the same page about what's needed in the game. All of us being given the same information at the same time is extraordinarily helpful.

Finally (and this question seems especially appropriate for you!), can you offer any advice to students reading this right now on a game design course somewhere?

I know this is going to sound cheesy, but think out of the box when designing a student project. As a student, there are really no risks to trying something new; there are no

publishers breathing down your neck, obligations to use a particular intellectual property, and so on.

In fact, if you're trying to be noticed, creating a copycat of a particular type of game is a huge risk. With a student project, everyone is pretty inexperienced; you have a very limited time to work on a project; you have no money; you generally have very few people; and on top of that by trying to create a clone of another game, you are basically asking others to compare your game to the original. Chances are the original game had a big budget, plenty of people working full-time on it, experienced professionals, and multiple years to create it in. So odds are, the comparison won't be terribly favourable for your student project.

Don't compete; innovate instead. As students, you are the next generation of game developers, so make our future a fun and bright one.

140

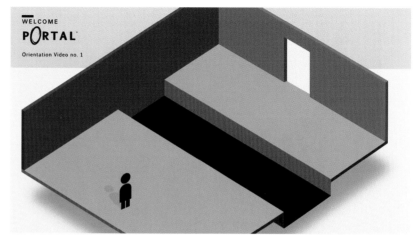

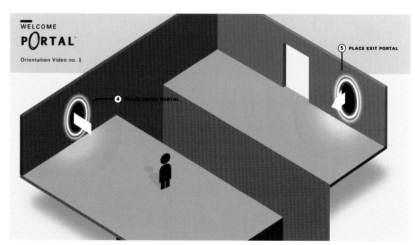

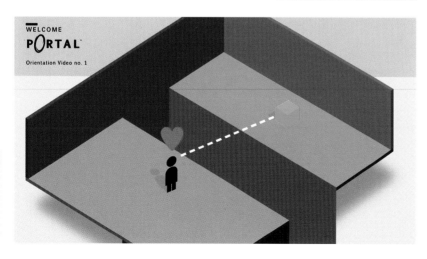

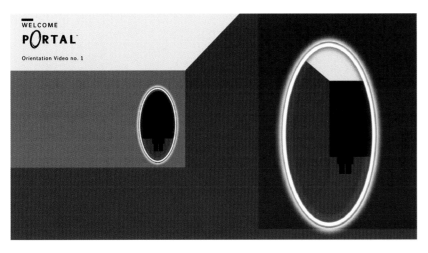

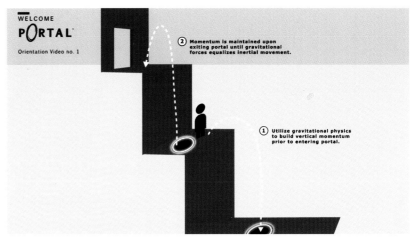

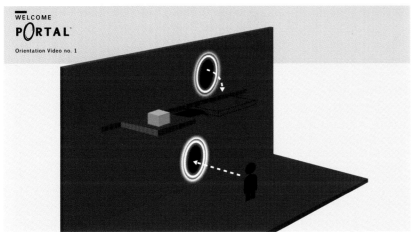

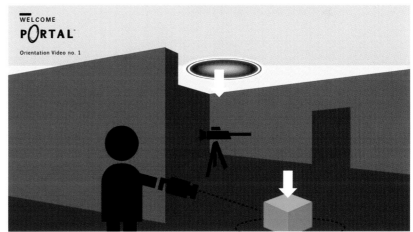

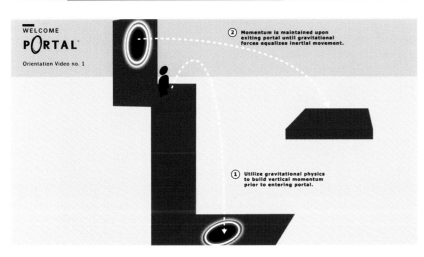

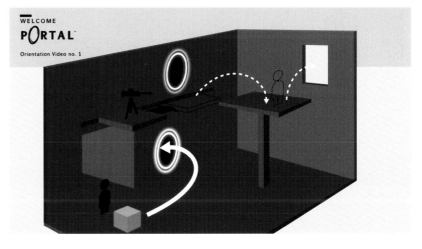

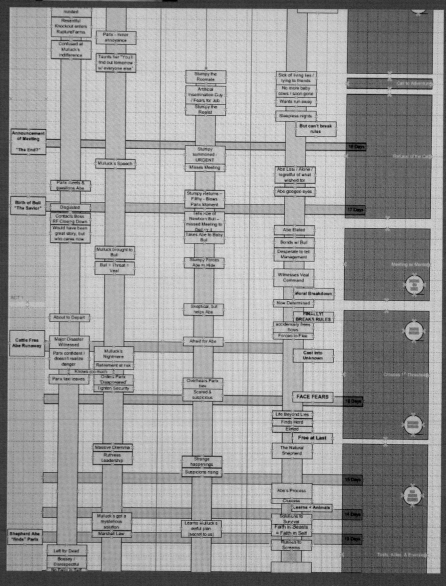

clockwise from top
1 Mission control in Lanning's studio.
2 Narrative flow plans for *Oddworld*.
3 Lanning at his desk.

LORNE LANNING (AFTERWORD)

www.oddworld.com

LOCATION
Berkeley, US

KEY TITLES
Oddworld: Stranger's Wrath (2005)
Oddworld: Munch's Oddysee (2001)
Oddworld: Abe's Exoddus (1998)
Oddworld: Abe's Oddysee (1997)

SELECTED AWARDS
Nominee, Outstanding Pre-Rendered Visuals in a Video Game,
    Stranger's Wrath (2006)
EDGE Magazine, Best Xbox of E3, *Munch's Oddysee* (2001)
AIAS Nominee, Adventure Game of the year, *Abe's Oddysee* (1998)

WHY BOTHER? SERIOUSLY. WHY MAKE VIDEOGAMES AT ALL? Lorne Lanning, having spent over a decade making the 'Oddworld' universe of games and receiving critical acclaim the world over, asked himself that question. In 2005, after the deeply troubled release of their fourth game, *Stranger's Wrath*, he and his partner Sherry McKenna announced they were closing down the 60-strong Oddworld studio and moving into different projects. In brief, they'd had enough of the industry.

Their new project, *Citizen Siege*, was announced in 2006. This is a full-length Hollywood CGI movie, directed by Lanning, and with a videogame not licensed from it but conceived as an integral part of this new imaginative universe. This is a new way to make entertainment, and it's one of the core points of this interview. Lanning and McKenna are finding new ways of creating interactive entertainment that are vitally important to anyone interested in making money from content.

Oddworld made some of the most beautiful and individual videogames ever released during its decade of production. Always at the front of any project, Lanning himself is one of the industry's few real stars. He's outspoken, opinionated and uncompromising in his views – but he delivers them with a West Coast charisma that demands the listener's attention. It's no accident he's returned to Hollywood.

Having discussed the who, how and where of game design, it seems right to end this book with some bigger questions. Why make games at all?

Tell me about the possibilities of game design – less what it is or what it isn't, but what it could be.

There seems to be a deficit in the vision pool – I believe!

Over and above the responsibilities to publishers and to players, what wider responsibilities do you think game designers have?

The simple answer is, to gamers and to games investors, which is pretty much the same answer we've heard from all industry through the last few centuries. Historically, industry

had recognized a responsibility to shareholders and somewhat to customers, but it's clear to us today that it failed to recognize its responsibility to the environment, to public health, and to so many other areas that have left us with the extremely challenging crises that face us today… with even greater challenges revealed when contemplating tomorrow.

But our problems came upon us as a result of collective denial and our relentless appetite for escape when faced with life and its challenges. Global warming, depletion of fisheries, polluted oceans, multinational interests mobilizing to own the world food and water supply, erosion of democracy and liberties of the many while handing increased power to an elite few under the guise of safety and protection. To many, it was obvious that all this was coming our way, but most of us chose not to pay attention. The more we pay attention, the longer the list grows and our physical landscape becomes more overwhelming and depressing.

So we don't want to think about how we live amongst industrial empires that own media conglomerates that routinely manufacture misinformation campaigns in the fight against hard science and anything else that conflicts with special interests and consumer appetites. It's not fun or easy for us to be informed about the pharmaceutical industry that is and has been systematically compounding world health crises by suppressing the spread of information that would otherwise inform the public of inexpensive cures – as was recently revealed by numerous Nobel Prize recipients.

When we look at the entertainment spectrum, we could argue that our responsibility is no different for the 21st century than it was in the 20th century. But we know now that we require deeper insights and motivations to help ensure that we avoid sustaining our habitual mistakes. Maybe it's time we try to create things more redeeming instead of just generating more crap atop the vast heap we're already wading through.

We know we have the ability to make interactive entertainment that serves the purpose of keeping someone entertained while proving profitable, but the question is, what are we *dumping* into the mindshare? Considering that

below The *Oddworld* games
communicated a strong environmental
agenda. Games as a provocation for
activism is a particular interest of
Lanning's.

144

games capture the greatest mindshare for any medium ever… what are we really doing with it? What is being passed along in the hours consumed in our artificial experiences?

When we consider the amount of mindshare that games are getting today, it becomes obvious that our medium has tremendous potential to make a difference. I look forward to the day we move beyond entertaining our audience and actually start inspiring and sensitizing our audience!

So as well as the well-documented apparent atrophy of the minds of gamers, what specific by-products of gaming do you have in mind?

To be clear, I think that there's a lot of healthy by-product too – which continues to be validated every day. For example, it's becoming more widely recognized that many industries and professions can benefit when their people play games. At a basic skill level, gaming has proven to improve dexterity and hand-to-eye co-ordination that helps not only the obvious military simulation skills but also scientists and surgeons and people in countless other fields. Social benefits are witnessed when individuals who might not otherwise be socializing and networking are enabled to do so because of online gaming. People who play connected games are proving that they display stronger teamwork skills in other educational- and career-oriented activities. Young people who play games are also displaying more faith in eventual success, and self-confidence, and are willing to try and fail more frequently than non-gamers. These are just a few of the benefits for game players as they make their way through the trials that come with living in a modern world.

It's important we don't exclude the positive benefits from discussion about games and their impact, because the games industry feels rather vulnerable, and for good reasons. The industry is frequently attacked by self-promoting politicians and religious zealot attorneys that see easy fodder and a quick way to get themselves visibility or make a quick buck – so it's a sensitive subject, and I don't want to ignore these sensitivities. However, this shouldn't deny our ability to discuss the uncomfortable – we should be intelligent enough to objectively analyze the pitfalls without having to fall on one side or another of a political spectrum.

The saddest thing I see in gaming is the popular trend that reprocesses war into pure entertainment. TV, film, radio, news… all media does this, but there's something particularly disturbing in that even contemporary war, fought at this very moment, is already shrink-wrapped and regurgitated as a fun product on the game shelf. Considering that the actual experience of those on the front lines is horrific and life-shattering, it somehow seems short-sighted that we manage to translate and reprocess these horrific events into something that is fun and enjoyable and void of the emotional devastation while trying to retain every other bit of detail to make the experience feel more real. Doesn't it seem reasonable that this trend is indirectly helping to desensitize the public to the realities of war?

On the upside, there are RTS [real-time strategy] games that have proven to increase user knowledge; players walk away with a better idea of what happened in history, yet they had fun while learning it. This is great. You'll hear teachers say their kids come into class and talk about their gaming experience and commenting, 'So *that's* what happened in the Byzantine empire!' They didn't pay attention in history class, but when they were invading the shorelines in a game they took interest and retained a beneficial history lesson. But as the trend moves to revisit history in more realistic first-person ways, we're also removing the horrors and collateral damage that would sicken us, that would never pass the ratings board for the largest demographic we're looking to target – and so we distill these distortions into a fun experience that is more likely to sell.

Now we see publishers sifting through the history of warfare to see what potentially viable wars can be turned into a watered-down, branded, interactive property. And most importantly… fun!

I think this may serve shareholders well in the short term, but in the big picture this type of diluted revisionism also serves to perpetuate pro-war propaganda – which is arguably amongst our biggest problems today, at least here in America.

A lot of game designers would return to the central concept of 'fun' as the core responsibility of the game designer.

Yes, and the free market is definitely driving that, when looked at from a statistical market research perspective. But let's think about it as a 'satisfying' experience – which doesn't necessarily mean fun – but means that it was *satisfying*, *engaging*, or possibly *compelling* on other psychological and emotional levels.

The deeper a good film is, the more we feel satisfied because we learned something, we feel satisfied because we saw a greater range of human dynamics or human passion, or saw truths that were currently hidden beneath the surface of our cover-story world – as in *The China Syndrome*, *Syriana*, *Apocalypse Now*, or so many other films that stick in our conscience for years to follow.

It's interesting that the films getting the most awards these days are those that are intellectually and emotionally challenging works of cinema, but in the game world we aren't tackling such issues. We are increasingly trapped in this idea that if the games aren't 'fun' by traditional standards – and don't fit within proven genres – then they can't succeed. But this is an extremely limiting paradigm and vision for the possibilities of an immensely potent medium, and it's a paradigm that is defined not by potential, but by insider perception and the result of retail conditions. However, it's not the *only* possibility, but so long as games exist at a price point of 50 dollars and gamers are required to make a several-hundred-dollar investment in a dedicated console to play titles, and the shelf life and retail conditions and development environments continue to get worse, then we're pretty much stuck in this non-innovating condition – even though there are alternatives that can lead to more compelling interactive entertainment.

A great example of this was *Myst*. It wasn't fun by game industry standards and, for that matter, neither was *The Sims*. *Myst* didn't have gameplay in the traditional sense beyond puzzle-solving and exploration. It wasn't action or competitive. But it was … experiential! The nature of its otherworldly, solitary, mysterious experience introduced a lot of people to gaming who had previously had no interest. *Myst* sucked them in, then they wanted more. But it never arrived, and they walked away from gaming wondering what happened to the experiences they might like.

What we have the opportunity to do now is create more sensitizing content that appeals to a wider range of human emotions and interest.

How optimistic are you about strategies for change?

I believe things can change, but with the development conditions the way they are and the expenses and risks involved, change has to come from different directions. If we look at the engineering philosophy of the hardware design of the next generation of consoles, and the reality of the production pipeline for the developers, there's a huge chasm between what they have to work with and what they really need. The development community doesn't need hardware systems that stifle innovation and give us half-assed tools and libraries that come with low-cost manufacturing manifestations that were designed in an engineering vacuum.

Every five years or so there's a new hardware transition. Some are worse than others, but as time goes on it's getting more and more unpleasant – and reliably. You're screwed if you invested 15 to 20 million dollars in a game that's just going to be on a PS3 at launch, because all you have is the possibility of selling a few hundred thousand units because that's *all* of the machines in the marketplace. Your game might be out there helping to sell more systems, but your chance to make a profit has been shot out from the realm of possibility. This is what happens when you exclude the people who make games from the design of the consoles. So if we want to see experiences evolve into something more innovative and daring, we've got to get away from the current tail-wagging-the-dog hardware dilemma and shift into an evolutionary philosophy that enables the development community to develop their tools with each subsequent console cycle. Currently, you dispose of your tools and are forced to make a steep investment in order to recreate them.

Digital distribution is a ray of hope in this regard, as is being proven by social networking sites, music distribution, MySpace, YouTube… anywhere where people are making creative products in their bedrooms yet finding a world

market. With this comes the possibility for new expansions in creative content to emerge.

This is a pretty bleak picture. Are you hopeful for your position within this business? Do you even want to work within it?

Well, we *want* to work with the games industry while not being limited by the conditions of it. From a practical business point of view, Sherry and I looked at the market and saw that a lot had changed. A lot of the incentives and motivations for birthing properties as games first have disintegrated for the small developer. However, if we approach property birthing differently by assessing what the landscape is now, then we increase the odds of creating greater market success on original IP. So how do we do that?

146

Well, first, we can't be in denial! We have to really assess the ugly part of industry conditions and figure out how to best approach new properties. We also have to follow our hearts with the stories we want to create.

Our strategy now is to launch as CG animated films first. If you can achieve this, then you can get the game to ride on the brand awareness that the movie marketing is creating through its larger marketing budget. The day for word-of-mouth promotion in the retail space has long since died and been buried for games. So if you don't have a publisher getting behind your titles properly, you cannot sell. And today, you have publishers not interested in promoting new intellectual properties they don't own or have a path to own.

What we're now focused on is birthing our new universe in a new way. A way that can be developed across game, film and TV in ways that haven't been possible before. But you really have to think in new ways to stand a chance of being

able to close this type of deal. Once you have what promises to be a hit movie, the game publishers are coming to you – you're not selling to them. So right now the publishers are going to Tony Hawk, Pixar, Peter Jackson. The people who are getting approached are the celebrity brand names or the larger market-proven storytellers. You think they're going around all the game designers? Nope! The best game designers in the world are all going around thinking 'what the hell's going on?' Why does Tobey Maguire get more ear-time from a game publisher than Warren Spector? The answer is… Tobey might be able to talk about the game on the *Today Show* or *Oprah*, but a hit-making game designer, he's not going to get us on *Oprah*. In today's climate, that's where the attention is. Game designers haven't been able to prove that they can get that kind of exposure, not even the most successful, including Will Wright or Miyamoto.

We want to tweak the odds to lean back towards the content creator. We own our properties because Sherry and I got into this business to achieve just that. We love and have breathed computer graphics for our entire careers. We don't have any kids because we see our kids as our CG creations and stories. In order to raise them well, we have to have creative controls on our content and some degree of control over their destiny. Nobody is going to raise your kids as well as you will. Using this metaphor, we can't hand off our children to strangers and just *hope* that they raise them well. When we started in this business, people were less concerned in the brand; they were interested in people who could make new, great games. They didn't believe that they had to own the property, they just thought they needed the distribution rights. The film industry didn't think that it needed the licensing rights, and then Lucas created *Star Wars*. He knew that if it was going to take off, people were going to want his T-shirts and toys and lunchboxes – but the film industry didn't even know that was possible. In his deal, he took less money up front in return for those rights and now he's a multi-billionaire. Without those deals, you wouldn't have ever heard of Lucas in the same light. We see it the same way but in a different climate.

Today, the real money is in the sequels. It's all about owning the brand. The games industry won't finance anything they don't own *unless* it's owned by someone else bigger who's going to be doing a bigger job of promoting it. But if you're still in the games industry thinking you want to be content creators who own your own property and have control over your creation's destiny, you're barking up a fruitless tree. It's just not going to happen, unless you start to birth those properties in other media first, not necessarily to the point of making them, but at least to the point where you have some financing and you can make deals in the game industry with very different terms.

Are there enough creatives in the games industry with the vision, or maybe the experience and ability to do that?

Maybe it's vision, maybe just moments of craziness. But you need that vision and crazy people in order to make things better. I think the more that the game developers can expand their vision of what they're doing, the better. Are they just making games, or are they really making worlds? The more they're able to be aware of the difference, the more potential they have to move into a larger spectrum of possibilities. How many game designers are capable of that today? Probably a relatively low number, but that number will inevitably increase as we head into the future.

A hybrid set of interests – people having a wide set of skills.

Right. And a problem with the higher education system at the moment is that schools are driven towards meeting the need to get students into specific jobs. Notions of developing skill sets like critical thinking and creativity come way down the line.

What are you proudest of?

I'm proudest of the fact that we birthed a property that managed to stand out in a number of ways. With its vision and art it influenced a lot of people to get more interested in art and games and world events and to get more involved with the world around them. For example, the Ministry of Education in Britain found that people who played *Oddworld* games showed a higher interest in getting involved in organizations like Amnesty. We have cases of people who found that the *Oddworld* games have helped people, and in one case actually saved a life. We're more proud of that than we are of how much money a game made. We're not about satisfying people's leisure time with uninspired content. We do what we do to inspire people and encourage them to have more influence on the world around them and rise to their full potential.

There are hopefully still some people reading this book who want to make videogames. What would you say to them?

If you just want to make money, you're talking to the wrong guy! But if you want to make a difference, then this is how I see it. We as people are creation generation machines that are capable of making things for the rest of the world that can make a difference. So, what difference is it that you are willing to work hard towards? It's easy to be a cog in a wheel and live a life of mediocrity, but our potential is much greater than that. We have the power as individuals to change the world if we put our hearts and minds to it. Games can and should be a powerful means for effecting change, so what is it that you care enough about that you'll work extra-hard to figure out how to make a difference with what you hope to create? Then, get ready to work harder than you've ever worked in your life and forget about a social life!

this spread Stills from the original
movie pitch for *Citizen Siege.*

GLOSSARY

AAA

Denotes a commercial game of high-quality, and high sales.

ALPHA

The software development stage preceding BETA. At this stage the game is in a playable state, but has many bugs.

BETA

The last phase of software development, prior to QA and manufacture. At this stage products are generally content-complete and all features are implemented. BETA stages may be open only to team members, or can also be open to invited members of the public.

BUG

A mistake in the software.

CUT SCENE

A non-playable cinematic element of a game, usually used for narrative exposition.

DEVELOPMENT CYCLE

The time from the beginning of development to final release.

E3

Acronym for Electronics Entertainment Expo, which was a large-scale event held in Los Angeles since 1995, providing a platform and focus for the launching of new videogame products to the world. After the third event in 2006, it was decided to scale the event down to a smaller, invitation-only event to be held in Santa Monica.

ENGINE

The core code which powers a game. Examples of popular engines might be 'Unreal' or 'Renderware'.

FIRMWARE

System-level software that operating systems use to talk to hardware.

FLOW

The optimal mental state identified by psychologist Mihaly Csikszentmihalyi, and in which the balance between the task presented and the person's ability to peform it is perfectly matched. Much game design is aimed towards acheiving this state in the player, this is more euphemistically described by gamers as 'being in the zone'.

FPS

Acronym for 'first-person shooter', which is a genre description of a type of game in which the onscreen viewpoint simulates the in-game player character's point of view.

GDC

Acronym for the Game Developers Conference, which is an annual event organized by CMP media, publishers of *Gamasutra* and *Game Developer* magazines. Hugely popular amongst the development community, it represents the platform where the industry comes together internationally to show and discuss work. Held in San Francisco since 2005, it was first held in 1987 by Chris Crawford in his living room.

GOLD

When software passes through Alpha, Beta and QA stages, and is ready for duplication and release to market, it is considered to have gone 'Gold'.

HD

Acronym for 'high-definition display technology', which is the buzzword of the seventh-generation of consoles, in particular Sony PS3 and X-Box 360. HD is actually a catch-all term for a wide variety of slightly different formats.

HUD

Acronym for 'heads-up-display', which is an on-screen visual display of important status information to the player. This is designed so as not to interfere with their view of the environment.

IP

Acronym for 'intellectual property', which means the non-physical assets of a company or individual. In game development terms, this can mean music, art, design documents, code – any element of the software. Such IP is fiercely protected.

LUDOLOGY

The study of games.

MIDDLEWARE

Software that developers sell or licence to other companies to aid in the development of third-party software.

MOD

Abbreviation of 'modifications', which in this sense are user-generated content items that have been developed for a specific videogame title. These can be as simple as altering in-game art and objects (such as *Simpsons Doom*) or as complex as fully-fledged levels in themselves (such as *Counter-Strike*). Since the popularity of Mod culture has exploded, many PC games are now designed with this ability in mind. Often titles ship with level-editing tools supplied as part of the software package. The commercial benefits of modding practice are self-evident, by encouraging and developing a platform for 'home-brew' development in their own products, developers and publishers propogate a high-degree of consumer loyalty. It should also be noted that Modding communities often prove to be a rich proving ground for designers, with some companies (most notably Valve) looking to these groups to source new staff.

MMORPG

Acronym for 'massively multiplayer online role-playing game', which is a genre of online game in which a large number of people interact with each other in a virtual world. This wildly popular genre of gaming is specifically both fictional and often narrative driven – as the title suggests. It is concerned with 'role-playing' in particular and shouldn't be confused with simply 'a lot of people playing together online'. Importantly, these worlds are persistent – they continue to exist and evolve when any single player is absent. As such, they are server based, hosted with the game publisher and are often thought of as services.

NEXT-GEN / NEXT-GENERATION

An unhelpfully time-sensitive term that alludes to the forthcoming iteration of videogame hardware technology. At time of writing and in this book, the term when used refers to the seventh generation of this technology. This began with the Microsoft Xbox 360 and also includes the Nintendo Wii and Sony PS3.

NDA

Acronym for a 'non-disclosure agreement', which is a legal contract binding the signatory to silence regarding any intellectual property they may have seen with regard to a specific project or company.

NPC

Acronym for 'non-player characters', which are software-controlled characters that appear within a game to populate environments. These can range from combat enemies to characters in place to provide explicit narrative exposition.

NTSC

The standard television format for North America and Japan (National Television Standards Council).

QA

Acronym for 'quality assurance', and the term used for the testing phase that follows the BETA development stage and precedes the game moving into manufacture.

PAL

The standard television format for Europe.

PATCHES

Small batches of code, usually distributed by the internet, which are applied to a piece of software to make it behave differently. Usually, these are bug-fixes or enhancements provided by developers but they can also be subversive code released by players.

PLATFORM

The hardware platform on which software is executed. For example, PC, Nintendo Wii, Playstation 3, X-box 360.

RPG

Acronym for 'role-playing games'. These games tend to have no particular winning or losing state; players inhabit the roles of fictional characters and participate in the game using a set of formal rules and systems. Within these rules, particularly imaginative play emerges. RPG's are very much a narrative-driven gaming experience.

RTS

Acronym for 'real-time strategy', which is a genre of strategy games, usually involving complex resource management and best exemplified by war games. Importantly, these games take place in a persistent 'real time' rather than being turn based.

SANDBOX

A genre of game where the player is encouraged to experiment with a given set of mechanics, often with no particular defined goal.

FURTHER READING

Books on Developers

Frontier Developments/David Braben

Spufford, Francis. *The Backroom Boys: The Secret Return of the British Boffin*. London: Faber and Faber, 2004.

Lorne Lanning

Johnson, Cathy and Daniel Wade. *The Art of Oddworld Inhabitants: The First Ten Years 1994 –2004*. Melbourne: Ballistic, 2004.

Valve

Hodgson, David S.J. *Half-Life 2: Raising the Bar*. Roseville, CA: Prima Games, 2006.

Game Design Theory

Crawford, Chris. *Art of Computer Game Design: Reflections of a Master Game Designer*. Berkeley: Osborne/McGraw-Hill, 1984.

———. *Chris Crawford on Game Design*. Upper Saddle River, NJ: Prentice Hall, 2003.

———. *Chris Crawford on Interactive Storytelling*. New Riders Series. Berkeley: Peachpit Press, 2004.

Curran, Ste. *Game Plan: Ten Designs That Changed the Face of Computer Gaming*. Brighton: Rotovision, 2004.

Curran, Ste, David McCarthy and Simon Byron. *The Complete Guide to Game Development, Art & Design*. Lewes: Ilex, 2005.

Koster, Ralph. *A Theory of Fun for Game Design*. Scottsdale, AZ: Paraglyph, 2004.

Salen, Katie and Eric Zimmerman. *The Game Design Reader: A Rules of Play Anthology*. Cambridge, MA: MIT Press, 2005.

———. *Rules of Play: Game Design Fundamentals*. Cambridge, MA: MIT Press, 2003.

Game Design Practice

Adams, Ernest and Andrew Rollings. *Fundamentals of Game Design (Game Design and Development)*. Upper Saddle River, NJ: Prentice-Hall, 2006.

Grossman, Austin, ed. *Postmortems from Game Developers*. San Francisco: CMP Books, 2003.

Game Business & Culture

Asakura, Reiji. *Revolutionaries at Sony: The Making of the Sony Playstation and the Visionaries Who Conquered the World of Video Games*. New York: McGraw-Hill Publishing, 2000.

Chaplin, Heather and Aaron Ruby. *SmartBomb! The Quest for Art, Entertainment, and Big Bucks in the Videogame Revolution*. Chapel Hill, NC: Algonquin Books of Chapel Hill, 2005.

Kushner, David. *Masters of Doom: How Two Guys Created an Empire and Transformed Pop Culture*. New York: Random House, 2003.

Poole, Stephen. *Trigger Happy: Videogames and the Entertainment Revolution*. New York: Arcade Publishing, 2000.

Takahashi, Dean. *Opening the XBox*. Roseville, CA: Crown Publications, 2002.

Game Studies

Atkins, Barry. *More Than a Game: The Computer Game as Fictional Form*. Manchester: Manchester University Press, 2003.

Bogost, Ian. *Unit Operations: an Approach to Videogame Criticism*. Cambridge, MA: MIT Press, 2007.

Aarseth, Espen. *Cybertext: Perspectives on Ergodic Literature*. Baltimore: John Hopkins University Press, 1997.

Kerr, Aphra. *The Business and Culture of Digital Games: Gamework and Gameplay*. London: Sage Publications 2004.

King, Geoff. *Tomb Raiders and Space Invaders: Video Games in the 21st Century*. London: I B Tauris & Co Ltd, 2005.

Newman, James. *Videogames*. London and New York: Routledge, 2004.

Newman, James and Iain Simons, eds. *Difficult Questions About Videogames*. Nottingham: Suppose Partners, 2004.

————. *100 Videogames*. London: BFI Publishing, 2007.

Rutter, Jason and Jo Bryce, eds. *Understanding Digital Games*. London: Sage Publications, 2004.

Websites

Developers

www.bizarrecreations.com (Bizarre Creations)
www.frd.co.uk (Free Radical Design)
www.freestylegames (FreeStyleGames)
www.frontier.co.uk (Frontier Developments)
www.gamedevblog (Jamie Fristrom's blog)
www.gastronaut.com (Gastronaut Studios)
www.harmonix.com (Harmonix)
www.introversion.co.uk (Introversion)
www.mediamolecule.com (Media Molecule)
www.monkeypoleclimb (Paul Carruthers)
www.oddworld.com (Lorne Lanning)
www.relentless.co.uk (Relentless Software)
www.toribash.com (Nabi Studios)
www.torpexgames.com (Torpex Games)
www.valvesoftware.com (Valve)

Online magazines

www.gamasutra.com
www.gdmag.com
www.next-gen.biz
wwww.oxm.co.uk

INDEX

Page numbers in *italics* refer to illustrations.

ACKNOWLEDGEMENTS

The author would like to express his sincere thanks to all of the participants in this book, whose generosity allowed it to happen. In addition thanks are due to Alison Beasley, Dr James Newman, Lucy Luck, Margaret Robertson, Chris Bridges, Paul Hough, Geri McCabe, Floyd Ferris, Christine MacSween, Hideotoshi Nakatsukasa, Doug Lombardi, Cathy Campos, Bill Dugan, Ben Ward, Sherry McKenna, Paul Gravett, Jo Lightfoot, Donald Dinwiddie, Jessica Spencer, Adam Hooper, Nicola Hodgson and Neil & Tim Russell.

Many thanks are also due to all who contributed images to this book. The credits for the images are as follows: (pp. 10–17) © Bizarre Creations/ Microsoft; (pp. 18–27) © Paul Carruthers, Monkey Sprites courtesy of Nick Lee and Steve Rowlands; (pp. 28–39) © Free Radical Design; (pp. 40–47) © Sony Computer Entertainment Europe, All Rights Reserved; (pp. 48–57) © Frontier Developments; (pp. 58–67) © Gastronaut Studios / Microsoft Game Studios; (pp. 68–77) © Harmonix Music Systems Inc.; (pp. 78–87) © Introversion Software; (pp. 88–99) all images © 2006 Sony Computer Entertainment Europe, All Rights Reserved; (pp. 100–5) © Nabi Studios Pte Ptd; (pp. 106–119) © Sony Computer Entertainment Europe, All Rights Reserved; (pp. 120–127) all images ©2007 NAMCO BANDAI Games Europe S.A.S.; (pp. 128–135) © Torpex Games, artwork by James Chao; (pp. 136–141) © Valve Software; (pp. 142–151) © Oddworld Inhabitants Inc.

Every effort has been made to contact the copyright holders, but should there be any errors or omissions, Laurence King Publishing would be pleased to insert the appropriate acknowledgement in any subsequent edition of this publication.